Quality Improvement in Education

Case Studies in Schools, Colleges and Universities

Edited by
Carl Parsons

David Fulton Publishers
London

David Fulton Publishers Ltd
2 Barbon Close, London WC1N 3JX

First published in Great Britain by
David Fulton Publishers 1994

Note: The right of Carl Parsons to be identified as the editor of this work has been asserted by him in accordance with the Copyright, Designs and Patents Act 1988.

British Library Cataloguing in Publication Data

A catalogue record for this book is available from the British Library

ISBN 1-85346-327-2

Typeset by RP Typesetters Ltd., Unit 13, 21 Wren Street, London WC1X 0HF.

Printed in Great Britain by the Cromwell Press, Melksham.

Contents

Preface

The idea for this book arose out of the work of part-time Masters students at Canterbury Christ Church College. They were studying on an M.Ed. module on the management of evaluation and quality assurance. There was such enthusiasm and exciting diversity of focuses, interests, interpretations and all-round debate amongst participants that it was obvious we had something novel to offer. The seven experienced teachers on the course who have contributed chapters to this collection have been joined by a number of other writers who have broadened the institutional focus and the geographical spread. All of the contributions are intended to be testimonies to people working, sometimes quite critically, at quality improvement measures. Of course, some of the authors are quite convinced of the value of quality improvement, and it has long been central to their work; others, through intellectual struggle, are new converts to TQM or an element within in it, but it is very much a perspective which derives from their analysis or the character of the institution in which they work.

It was an ambitious programme to try to contain within the covers of a single volume quality assurance case studies which span infant school to university and on to adult training. Yet there can be something quite disturbing about concentrating on quality, the enrichment of experience and the improvement in learning that limits itself to one type of institution or one level of education.

The delight in putting the book together stems from the commitment shown by the individual authors, the sturdy debate that led to the final offerings and also the tolerance of diversity and scepticism within the group of authors. The hope of the authors is that this volume can be something of a companion to others working at the quality management business. The book may save some people a little time in providing ideas about instruments and techniques that can be applied. It may help some people avoid some of the pitfalls that others will have encountered. It may inspire people to adopt their own style of quality management borrowing from whatever is useful to make the best set-up for their own institution. It may give confidence; it may help to show that this whole movement, serious though it is, effective though we hope it may be, has its light-hearted side too, as any element of life should have. The variety of approaches and the quality in the human endeavour represented in these chapters should also represent quality assurance management as containing within it huge variety from the deeply technocratic and mechanistic to something which is as warmly human as we would want it to be.

Contributors

Paul Barras is Deputy Head Teacher, St. John Fisher School, Chatham, Kent. As an Education Manager he has practical and theoretical interests in quality, and has as one of his responsibilities in the school, an oversight of assessment policy and practice.

Kevin Buckley is Deputy Head Teacher, Cliftonville County Primary School, Kent. He has concerns about school/home relationships and how, in the situation where schools compete for pupils, the relationship with parents may be developed into a 'partnership' to raise quality.

Glen Cannon is Head Teacher, White Oak Junior School, Swanley, Kent. Applying TQM and consulting the customer are developments to which Glen Cannon and his school are committed. The 'total' in TQM means most definitely for him that governors and staff are also central participants.

John Chesterton works for Design 2 Distribution (D2D) ICL Ltd. He is an experienced trainer in the applications of TQM to education, and has run workshops all over the country.

Philip Cox is Head of Quality Management at De Montfort University. He has been instrumental in introducing and disseminating through the University a strategic approach to quality maintenance and enhancement which has attracted national and international interest.

Les Franklin is Programme Leader at East Birmingham College. He has a particular interest in equal opportunities and quality management, and has been able to document the humanistic quality improvement trends at East Birmingham College.

Robert Green, Senior Assistant Registrar at the University of Southampton, has been instrumental in negotiating the university's academic quality assurance policy and procedures through the university's committees and the Association of University Teachers. The Assessment of Departmental Academic Performance Committee established at the University of Southampton has an eye both to sensitive management of the quality procedures within the University, and seeing that these conform with demands made by external bodies for quality information.

Myrna Harris is a Teacher of English and Drama at Haberdasher's Aske's School for Girls, Hertfordshire, and has a commitment to applying quality concepts and practices in creative areas of education. She is committed to the promotion of both creativity and discipline in A Level Theatre Studies. Her selection from and adaption of TQM involves all significant stake holders and allows them all a share in the joy of effective learning in a creative sphere.

Mary Healy is Quality Manager at King Harold Grant Maintained Secondary School, Waltham Abbey, Essex. Her work in the quality area in the school stretches back to institutional planning and school effectiveness review and the momentum of her work continues through British Standards Registration.

Ruth Hendry is a Year 2 Class teacher at Priory County Infants' School, Ramsgate. Her concern for raising standards at Key Stage I has led her to investigate assessment and recording practices in her school.

Hugh Koch runs his own consultancy service based in Cheltenham and is concerned with quality management in all public sector services. He has written extensively on TQM in healthcare, and has extensive experience in running workshops both in this country and abroad.

Carl Parsons is a Reader in Teacher Education and Quality Review and Enhancement Officer at Canterbury Christ Church College. He has extended a long-standing interest and expertise in evaluation in education into the field of Quality Management. He recently passed the Institute of Quality Assurance's Quality Assurance Management exam. His current interest is in the manageability and utility of quality procedures within organizations.

Keith Sanders is Manager of Kent Training Centres, Dover. He has experience of organizing his centre's successful application for BS 5750 registration. Though seeing BS 5750 registration as essential in a fiercely competitive training market he is aware of the limitations and dangers it brings with it.

Keith Sharpe is Director of the BA(Ed) programme at Canterbury Christ Church College. He has been instrumental in bringing a routine of student course evaluation as part of a series of quality control procedures to a large four year undergraduate programme of initial teacher education.

Heather Speller is Manager of the Curriculum and Quality Assurance Development Unit at South Kent College. She supports and coordinates a range of in-house improvement strategies including Investors in People. Her major interests are in quality development in the FE sector.

Phil Stephenson is a member of the East Sussex Special Educational Needs Development team. He is an experienced trainer and has worked to establish systems for the design and delivery of courses and workshops to teachers, ancillaries and governors that are of maximum effectiveness.

Robert Whatmough is Deputy Head Teacher at Chapter School, Strood in Kent. He has a keen interest in the concepts of TQA and a selective approach to their application in a secondary school. He has a particularly critical perspective upon the concept of quality in education or caring services and the role of customers' judgements of quality.

Chapter 1
The Politics and Practice of Quality

Carl Parsons

Introduction

Quality assurance management systems have been in existence for decades. The military set up procedures early in the century to try to ensure that suppliers delivered ammunition and weapons that were up to standard. Currently organizations that buy in components, materials or services from other producers or suppliers employ systems to ensure that those businesses are run in such a way as to minimize the possibility of faulty goods or deficient services being delivered. It is at the very least interesting to note the role of the military until very recently in the quality business: the Institute of Quality Assurance and the British Quality Association had retired brigadiers and rear admirals on their boards or councils. As the biggest procurer over the years of quality assured goods and services the domination of the forces should be no surprise. The NHS may, in more recent times, have become the biggest buyer. It seems better somehow to have quality assurance associated with improving and saving lives rather than with efficient killing! The British Quality Association, now the Federation, has a responsibility for running the National Quality Awards and the whole quality push has definitely moved from the military to the industrial and commercial. The inroads it has made into the education sector come largely from this quarter with TECs instituting procedures to audit and inspect colleges and training centres to which contracts are awarded. FE colleges are going for BS 5750 certification as a requirement for getting business from firms who are themselves required to have quality assurance registration.

As from 1 August 1994, BS 5750 becomes BS EN ISO 9000 (British Standards, 1994), with some changes in the clauses and standards statements. All this brings it more explicitly in line with the international standard, but the essentials remain the same and

ISO 9000

discussions in this and later chapters about BS 5750 remain stub-
bornly relevant.

Expensively produced, yet free, booklets have been available from
DTI on such topics as *The Quality Gurus* (DTI, 1992a) and *Total
Quality Management and Effective Leadership* (DTI, 1992a) along
with a series of videos, also free. These are not directed at education
but the advice must be to draw on quality wisdom wherever you can
find it.

Against such a background this chapter has four purposes:

1. to define quality assurance and associated terms;
2. to review existing quality assurance management systems and
   frameworks;
3. to examine the recent origins of, and the responses to, quality
   assurance demands;
4. to develop a constructively critical view of quality management,
   whether partial quality management or total quality management.

Defining Quality

Quality is 'the totality of features and characteristics of a product
or service that bear on its ability to satisfy stated or implied needs'
(British Standards, 1987a). This covers fitness for purpose and
satisfying customer needs.

Quality control is the 'operational techniques and activities that
are used to fulfil requirements for quality' (British Standards,
1987a).

Quality assurance is all the planned and systematic actions necessary to provide adequate confidence that a product or service will
satisfy given requirements for quality.

Quality audit is a check to see if the quality system exists and
operates as claimed.

Quality assessment is making a judgement about the standards
reached by an organization.

A quality assurance management system (QAMS) directs attention
to the appropriate quality assurance controls that can be applied in
all key areas and to all stages of supply of the product or service.
This is to ensure that the processes involved in providing the
product or service have been quality assured. The aims of a
QAMS are to prevent non-conformity or customer problems and
to achieve customer satisfaction; the objectives are to minimize
risk and cost and maximize benefits that can be obtained from
achieving the required quality standards (Vorley, 1991, p. 10)

A Standard Quality Assurance Management System: British Standards 5750

The best-known QAMS is the BS 5750 certification scheme which directly parallels the Geneva-based International Standards Organization's ISO 9000. The scheme has 18 or 20 sections, depending on whether the enterprise invents or designs its own product or service. British Standards have brought out advisory documents showing how the scheme, originally designed for manufacturing, could apply to services and, indeed, there is a specific advisory document for education. BSI certification is not an indicator that an institution is a quality institution but that it has procedures in place to check, control and assure quality. Table 1.1 sets out the sections that have to be satisfied and many of these can be readily interpreted into a form applicable to an educational setting. Freeman (1993) offers very helpful guidance for educational institutions applying for BS 5750.

Table 1.1 ISO 9000/ BS 5750 quality standard categories

4.1 Management responsibility
4.2 Quality system
4.3 Contract review
4.4 Design control
   (Part 1 only unless the product or service is unique, i.e. invented by the institution)
4.5 Document control
4.6 Purchasing
4.7 Purchaser supplied product
4.8 Product identification and traceability
4.9 Process control
4.10 Inspection and testing
4.11 Inspection, measuring and test equipment (sometimes called 'calibration')
4.12 Inspection and test status
4.13 Control of non-conforming product
4.14 Corrective action
4.15 Handling, storage, packaging and delivery
4.16 Quality records
4.17 Internal quality audits
4.18 Training
4.19 Servicing (Part 1 only unless contract agreement requires follow-up)
4.20 Statistical techniques

Source: (BSI,1987b)

Some authors (e.g., Vorley, 1991) actually suggest that other focuses should be part of a quality system also. These include after-sales servicing, as in 4.19 above, market reporting, product safety and reliability, motivation (of the work force) and economics (the cost of achieving quality or the cost of poor quality).

The benefits of certification are said to be various, and include:

- a fully documented system which informs *insiders* about the organization and systems for documentation, quality checks and support;
- documentation that is very useful for the induction of newcomers;
- it points out the gaps in procedures, areas of uncertainty, areas where data should be available and where checks should be made regularly;
- it gives a sense of control, i.e. it sets out important aspects of how the work of the organization should be run and what records there are that it is being run according to the plan (being *out of control* simply means not being quite sure what is going on);
- a documented system to assure (impress?) outsiders; it is powerful in presenting to outside bodies which have a stake in the organization (DfE, FEFCE, HEFCE, HEQC) that it is run well and that, consequently, there is little need to check the organization thoroughly themselves – the *Let's Do It To Ourselves Before They Do It To Us* syndrome! (Parsons,1992);
- it can provide the basis for a total quality management approach.

The drawbacks are less about the expense of setting up and maintaining the system – though certification *is* expensive – than with the language and structure of the system and the fact that it does not apply naturally to education.

Lesser and Partial Quality Assurance Management Systems

The Management Charter Initiative (MCI), formed in 1988, is a non-profit making organization funded by subscription from the private and public sector and a grant from the Employment Department. Its goal is 'to improve the performance of UK organisations by improving the quality of UK managers' (Management Charter Initiative, 1992). The key focus here is management effectiveness.

The Investors in People (IIP) programme, also until recently Employment Department-funded, has goals which relate to staff development and attention to staff attitudes and commitment. Local Training and Enterprise Councils (TECs) carry out the registration and offer free consultancy to help organizations meet the criteria. There is an initial questionnaire provided which is designed to gauge current manager and staff attitudes, the degree to which staff feel consulted and their involvement in staff development of all sorts. Examining this questionnaire is an education in itself. Those who are put off by it need to realize that you don't have to use it. The key focus for IIP is valuing and developing staff.

School self-evaluation has been the major, albeit limited, means by which quality in schools was supposedly assured. It took various forms, from action research (see CARN publications, 1977 onwards), to very open-ended 'professional' approaches as reported by Simon (1987) and in the Schools Council-funded 'Teacher-Pupil Interaction and the Quality of Learning' project (see Altrichter *et al.*, 1993). More structured whole-institution efforts such as GRIDS (Abbott *et al.*, 1988) or DION (Elliott-Kemp and Williams, 1980) grew from this but somehow seemed to miss convincing the public (if they cared) or the national decision-makers and funding sources. The key focus in these schemes is a liberal, professional collegiality.

The requirements for Institutional Development Planning have become ever firmer. The central government pressures are evident through advisory documents (DES, 1989, 1991), and inspection and audit frameworks (HEQC, 1992; OFSTED, 1993) plainly point to an assessment made of an institution's quality assurance procedures and practices. TQM *may* link together all of the existing systems to meet current demands!

Greater than a Quality Assurance Management System: Total Quality Management

Total quality management has arrived like an apocalypse on the educational scene. It comes, as many of these touching fashions do, from America via the East bringing with it the quiet fervour of low-church evangelism and the mystique of yoga. It is a way of life.

TQM is about *everyone* working to improve *all aspects* of an organization's functioning. One definition is 'Continuously meeting agreed customer requirements at the lowest cost, by releasing the potential of all employees' (TQM International, 1992). It involves a distinct sort of culture, communication and commitment with systems, tools and teams. There is a sense of ultimate service which goes beyond mission and vision to practical steps which lead to the 'helix of never ending improvement' (ibid.).

TQM is a rather spiritual response to such practical pressures but it has a significant following and is all the more seductive in these barren, charmless times (for education) precisely because of its strong affective dimension. TQM faces crude demands for evidence of quality with serenity, confidence in technical competence and a moral assurance which lifts it above the fray.

For TQM believers there is a sort of magical delight in working towards the unknowable – what true excellence will look and feel like. There is the promise of fulfilment signalled by feedback from those totally satisfied customers, if you only have faith. The movement brings an impressive array of joyous religiosity which includes the following:

prophets	– *gurus*
liturgies	– *Crosby's (1986) four absolutes of quality management*
	– *the 14 steps to quality improvement*
a Protestant	– *Feigenbaum's (1983) ten crucial benchmarks*
discipline with	– *statistical techniques*
Eastern mystique	– *prevention not detection*
sin	– *Deming's (1988) deadly diseases*
iconography	– *Ishikawa's (1985) fishbone diagrams*
	– *charts and histograms*
the ultimate	– *continuous quality improvement*
which is	*in a total quality environment*
attainable in this world	– *total customer satisfaction*
spiritual depth	– *Deming's (1988) Theory of profound knowledge*
	– *Juran's (1988) Breakthrough*
high moral tone	– *zero defects*
mixed with	– *right first time*
ecstasy	– *involve everyone*
	– *delighting the customer*
	– *a passion (Peters, 1989) or obsession (Deming, 1988) with quality*
salvation	– *reduced waste, bigger market share, raised esteem, survival.*

This is not to mock. Attractive, even idealized, goals are no bad things. Ritual is much underrated as a part of professional life and too often the charismatics whom we have looked up to, but who have operated under no particular system, have not shown us the way.

There is a strong affective dimension in any change process and while in TQM there is an emphasis on the responsibility that each person has for quality, it is within a nurturing, non-threatening culture where people operate in teams aware of the support they must give to others.

It's full of slogans too such as one sees outside the Baptist Chapel – 'Quality is Free' (Crosby, 1986); 'Those who are not dissatisfied will never make any progress' (Shingo, 1985). 'Do the right thing! Do it right!' (Juran, 1988). We even have the Ten Commandments of Quality (Balano, 1994). It is the absolutes which hit one – *total* quality, *zero* defects, *world class* performance and right *first* time. Mix this with passion, obsession and devotion backed by Deming's (1988) profound knowledge and we confront a highly emotive, high principled belief system. As a quasi-religion it is enticingly swash-buckling and full of hope and togetherness.

The aged sages that bestride the TQM field are impressive: at the time of writing, Juran is 89 and still going strong; Deming died in December 1993 at the age of 93 and a fortieth Anniversary edition of Feigenbaum's *Total Quality Control* (1983) has been published. Their personal staying power as well as the continuing currency of their books must mean something.

There are also the born-again, the sceptics and even the false prophets – usually the consultants waiting on the side to make a quick profit helping your organization move from tentative spiritual conversion to a new practical way of life.

Of course it is really all very secular. There are prizes for quality or excellence; the Malcolm Baldridge National Quality Award exists in the USA and last year King Juan Carlos presented the first batch of European Quality Awards. There is an insignia for registering with British Standards, a stamp for having a Charter or a laurel for having successfully implemented an Investors in People programme.

This is a loosely connected church with considerable variety in it. All are united in the commitment to a customer orientation but in a way which reduces its narrow commercial and, therefore, rather profane emphasis; it sees us all who are internal to an organization having a customer-supplier relationship and that this chain or network must be made to operate well.

One might well ask whether the congregation in British education will be converted to the new religion. People in education tend to be wary of emotive fads. Several of the chapters in this volume describe the selective and pragmatic use of techniques and ideas drawn from TQM; Whatmough (Chapter 10) and Stephenson (Chapter 14) offer a well-argued restrained position. Some feel that TQM is all right for those in manufacturing or in retail. Some say it is ok for the secretarial staff and support staff in a school, university or college. Professionals and intellectuals still believe all too often in brute sanity even when all the evidence shows it does not bring about change. Perhaps they will find it's time they allowed the affective, the spiritual even, to join with the cognitive in generating improvement. There may be delight and ecstasy in this communal endeavour following a scheme tailored to the institution's needs and character. Franklin's chapter on East Birmingham College (Chapter 12) communicates a touch of that.

Research has shown that large numbers of TQM projects, like quality circles before them, have failed (Hill, 1991; Robson, 1988). There is the warning given against naive implementation of the ideas and techniques of TQM. If these are heeded and a robust, resourced approach, backed by the most senior of management, is set in motion then the benefits are considerable as John Chesterton in Chapter 3 argues. There may be much in the trans-Atlantic, trans-Pacific mix of stars and stripes and Nintendo, Gospel and Zen. People find surprisingly palatable the ideas of our all being suppliers and customers in a chain, schemes for identifying and remedying deficiencies and roles for quality improvement teams and exercises.

Educational institutions, confronted by the challenge of doing more with less under greater scrutiny, can use TQM. Robustly shaped to the sort of service education, at all levels, sets itself to provide, TQM can help to meet external demands and generate favourable internal climates. It requires the communication of a shared vision from the most senior. It requires commitment and team-work. It requires new roles, structures and processes that will make some educational institutions gasp a little.

There may be no miracles or millennium but TQM speaks not just of improved efficiency and effectiveness but of a better way of work life. In these hard times in education many would settle for that as a form of salvation.

A Professional Model of Quality Assurance

Education and health *may* be different to industry and commerce, but managers in any of these spheres are not going to forget that achieving complete customer satisfaction helps an organization to survive and profit. Professional and specialist training may mean that the customer is not the overriding judge of what constitutes quality.

Øvretveit (1992) presents in relation to the health service a more sophisticated view of *quality* which has direct application to the education service. Øvretveit defines three dimensions of quality which, redefined for education, might take the following form:

l   *client quality:* what customers (pupils and parents) and clients (employers, community) want from the service;
/   *professional quality:* whether the service meets needs as defined by professional providers and whether it correctly carries out techniques and procedures which are believed to be necessary to meet client needs;
l   *management quality:* the most efficient and productive use of resources within limits and directives set by higher authorities.

This account combines the commercially dominant view of customer satisfaction with acknowledgement of the rights, duties and judgements of professionals and with an acceptance of budget limits and control by government departments, to which public employees must, to a degree, be subject.

Realism in Quality Assurance Management

More important than the name given to the quality system an institution chooses is the fact that quality is on the agenda, that it has a high public profile within the institution and that there is an operational dimension which results in identifiable, perhaps measurable, benefits for providers and customers.

Three final notes to end this chapter concern prosperity, control and democracy. First, one must acknowledge the similarities which exist between education and businesses; institutions that can offer services and products of proven quality can charge more, are awarded more, can be sure of raised public esteem and will prosper – in so far as the macro-economic situation will allow. Second, the trend certainly feels like deprofessionalization; professionals are taking on the rather mechanistic and starched clothes of others because they *have* to be worn, but it may not be for ever and inspection, such as we will all be subject to, is expensive and itself a target for cuts. Third, moderated self-assessment may one day be a position to be won back; the autonomy once experienced, called professional 'despotism' by Taylor (1969), may not ever be attainable again – nor desirable in a democratic society.

Chapter 2

Quality Improvement in Action

Carl Parsons

Introduction

Education professionals have always claimed to pay attention to quality. This assertion has rested largely on faith in professional training ensuring that courses are well designed, well taught and rigorously assessed. Monitoring quality and policing the work of the membership is inherent in the definition of 'professional' (Etzioni, 1969) yet is exercised only in medicine and the law, even then rather dubiously. This is not something achieved in education; there is no Teaching Council on the horizon. That leaves something of a vacuum in terms of control and responsibility.

The rather liberal developments in self-evaluation and action research that took place in schools years ago under the Schools Council (Tawney, 1974) and latterly independently or with LEA guidance (Elliott, 1982) were never going to win public confidence because of the professional introversion they exuded. It is interesting to observe now the alacrity with which education professionals are using 'off-the-shelf' models. This is clearly happening in schools (see Chapters 7 and 8), with alacrity at FE level (see Chapters 11, 12 and 13) and in universities (Chapters 17 and 18). The realism of the paymasters, in the accountability-oriented quality assurance systems they produce, is undeniable. Ignore this realism at your peril.

Self-evaluation and action research were always in the past the preserve of the philosophically over-committed few and they have been overtaken by a managerial prerogative which has seen BS 5750 brought in, schemes for adapting the OFSTED inspection framework so that you do it to yourself before they arrive, and similar adaptations made to the HEQC audit framework and to the HEFCE quality assessment framework. Educationists have given up ownership to implement a system that, while it will be useful for themselves, will protect them from outsiders.

The cases reported in this volume extend from examples in primary education, secondary schools through further education, in-service training and on to higher education. The primary school initiatives are small-scale and focused. In the secondary sector they are, in some cases, more ambitious but mostly still piecemeal, though certainly more aware of imminent OFSTED inspection. In FE colleges off-the-shelf approaches are more obvious. In HE, academic freedom might have gone but institutions' command of their internal quality systems is conveyed in an assured manner, in some cases as though warts do not exist, and outside auditors and assessors should beware because these houses are in order. It is the variety, where some quality approaches serve internal interests and others have a wary eye on the outside inspections, that is the fascination.

BS 5750 and IIP

The British Standard for quality management, BS 5750, and its international parallel, ISO 9000 are *the* standard. Investors in People is the other highly publicized approach though this focuses mainly on staff training. Chapters 7, 12 and 13 report on experiences of gaining BS 5750. It is worth noting that a number of institutions have explored the BS 5750 route and, in travelling some way along it, have decided it has done them enough good without going for certification itself and all the expense that is entailed. If your institution is going for certification the advice is to shop around; awarding bodies vary and so do the prices they charge. The National Accreditation Council for Certification Bodies, based in London, can give a list of organizations able to audit quality systems and issue accreditation and there may be others, nearly accredited by NACCB, which may be cheaper as they are fighting to get into the market. One FE college estimated that preparation for certification cost £70,000 (Sandwell, 1992). Direct costs to BSI would be about £5,000 for an organization with 250 employees; this would involve about nine person-days for the initial audit of the system, carried out by external quality auditors, and about £3,000 annually for continuing the certification with six-monthly audits of parts of the system.

An education or training institution going the BS 5750 route may turn to a consultant for support though, for the bold, there are a number of books which set out to provide the necessary advice (Freeman, 1993; Jackson and Ashton, 1993; Waller *et al.*, 1993).

Healy (Chapter 7) and Sanders (Chapter 13) indicate that BS 5750 certification is not the end of the matter – nor should it be. The cautions they offer are that it has to be quality assurance of a system that you really are working, not something created for the quality assessors, and that everyone has to understand it. As Sanders says, it can be an inhibitor in that once you have devised your manual and had it approved, you might be very wary about changing anything. For Healy and Franklin (Chapter 12) the move forward is to TQM. British Standards has its own total quality standard now, BS 7850 (BSI, 1992). Waller *et al.* (1993) urge us on with the following:

> After gaining ISO9000 registration, organisations need to make sure that they don't stand still and that there is a continuing drive towards higher levels of quality. The process of looking beyond the requirements of ISO9000 registration to the wider quality needs of the organisation is called Total Quality Management (p.11).

Maybe it is. An interesting article by Corrigan (1994) is entitled 'Is ISO9000 the path to TQM? Even if it isn't, it can't hurt', and that is probably the spirit to take it in. Whether an organization tries to gain BS 5750 certification or not, tremendous use can be made of the discipline that comes from considering it. The manual, standardizing procedures, the notions of non-compliances, non-conforming products and corrective action are very helpful.

Speller, Chapter 11, draws the connections between Investors in People, BS 5750 and TQM, and quotes Sheppard (1992) on people being at the heart of quality. 'Investors', as the standard is coming to be known familiarly amongst the converted, is being promoted strongly in education. It is reported that 70 per cent of further education establishments have committed themselves to working towards registration and 50 have achieved it (*Insight,* 1994, p.4). Mary Chapman, the first chief executive of IIP UK Ltd, speaks of the importance of focusing on the quality of the work force – and improving that quality: 'Investors is focussed on the quality of people in an organisation – the better the quality of the people, the better the results they will achieve' (ibid).

Speller gives a feel for what it is like to be en route to the quality standard, the motives that made them choose IIP and some of the minor disappointments on the way that you must not allow to be too discouraging. The way forward to TQM, should it be chosen by the college, seems pretty straightforward from the four principles of IIP – commitment, planning, action and evaluation.

TQM: Culture and Environment

John Chesterton in Chapter 3 outlines benignly the benefits that TQM offers to schools. Working in quality in D2D (Design to Development) in ICL and contributing to Careers Research and Advisory Centre (CRAC) courses on quality, his experience is extensive. His fine-tuning to education is certainly aided by having a spouse in secondary education. The depth and breadth of vision presented in Chapter 3 keeps the focus very much on the main business of the enterprise – educating children – and improvements sought in the operation of the organization are to serve that end. Pecking away at small bits of the problem is a fair enough way to start – addressing a non-conformance here and a recognized deficiency there – but its contribution to the attainment of the overall objectives of the enterprise should always be in sight, and this contribution should be monitored. Schools may not follow Chesterton headlong into Total Quality Improvement (TQI), Total Quality Environment (TQE), Total Quality Commitment (TQC) or Success Through Quality (STQ). Statistical process control and benchmarking may not have immediate allure and yet we are aware of the dangers of an approach to it all which is too piecemeal. Mary Healy (Chapter 7) and Les Franklin (Chapter 12) report on institutions that have been at it longest and appear to be reaching, and receiving motivation from, those less tangible levels of ethos, culture and commitment. Rooting a system of quality management at that level is something to be worked at and there are certainly signs of strong movement in this direction in the initiatives reported by Buckley (Chapter 5), Cannon (Chapter 6) and Barras (Chapter 8). The use that Buckley (Chapter 5) and Harris (Chapter 9) make of quality circles holds attractions; Buckley's Quality Street Gang may take off as a new concept in its own right if it succeeds in satisfying the participants as well as the customers. Whatmough's inclusion of students into what approximated to a quality circle set-up (Chapter 10), is another development worth considering.

The importance of teams and the principle that everyone must accept that quality is their business are points that both Healy and Stephenson (Chapter 14) make. Stephenson's 'Right second time' may not be such a departure from the absolutes of TQM since he means that his in-service training courses will be right second time *and forever after that.*

Those interested in TQM should certainly read Koch's chapter (16); it is a healthy sign (from the health industry!) that there are notions, guidelines, techniques, frameworks and cautions that can be borrowed, with little need for reinterpretation, for use in education. Training teachers to manage learning may have few important differences from managing healthcare workers. Koch's flowchart, pillars and pyramids are part of a thoroughbred, high-flying quality programme. It is a challenging theoretical injection as the end of the book is approaching. Though so much of what we see in TQM is diagrams and slogans, if it can accomplish for a workforce Deming's goal, 'Work smarter, not harder', it will have served producers and consumers alike. One hopes that there will be, in Franklin's terms (Chapter 12) more laughing and loving, and less crying.

OFSTED, FEFCE, HEQC and HEFCE

OFSTED (The Office for Standards in Education), FEFCE (The Further Education Funding Council for England), HEQC (The Higher Education Quality Council) and HEFCE (The Higher Education Funding Council for England), with their Welsh, Scottish and Northern Irish counterparts, are a powerful presence on the quality scene.

TQM entices top management's approval and support. The prospect of inspection and assessment from external agents sees top management taking the lead from the start. Institutions are readily taking on the external quality assurance frameworks and applying them to themselves. And why not? It would be silly to have a home-made quality assurance framework which did not cover key areas on which the institution is to be assessed. Experts certainly put the framework together for these governmental agencies. It is another area of life where plagiarism is a good thing and inspection agencies actually expect this backwash effect from their procedures.

Hendry, in Chapter 4, wants to raise the quality of the school's assessment system at Key Stage 1. Making consistent use of Willie (1992) and West-Burnham (1992), she works with staff to identify weaknesses and address them so that OFSTED inspection criteria in that area are met.

In Paul Barras' chapter, looking at the school's assessment, reporting and recording (ARR) policy, there is evidence of backwash upon backwash; ARR is a category in the OFSTED (1993) *Handbook for Inspection* and, borrowing for the school the terminology and focusing upon the components in OFSTED terms, led to at least one department urgently reviewing its own ARR before the school's own audit of this area, which in turn was to precede the official OFSTED inspection.

More headteachers and others are now going on the OFSTED inspection training courses and, indeed, are being encouraged by OFSTED to do so. Many are motivated by a desire to know the system from the inside – pheasants turned gamekeepers.

The extent of the official fostering of this backwash effect may be gauged by this extract from one of many case studies displayed with approval in a recent OFSTED publication:

'Each year 4% of lessons are observed by senior management. Success depends on 80% being judged 'sound' or better. Similarly, each week, the work of 6 pupils from each year group is scrutinised, again using the yardstick of 80% 'sound' or better. In addition, one whole class set of books is also examined on the same basis. The school had committed itself to a 25% reduction in poor work ...' (OFSTED, 1994).

The FEFCE (1993) approach to inspection does not figure significantly in the two chapters here on the FE sector (Chapters 11 and 12). It could be that this sector has been so beleaguered by quality assessments over the years and had to be so sensitive to the market anyway that, with recent 'incorporation', new inspection procedures hold no new fears.

Higher education institutions will also have to satisfy paymasters that courses and other services are being provided to a certain standard. Models recommended for HE resemble closely BS 5750. The Engineering Professors' Conference (Burge and Tannock, 1992) have produced a scheme which is moderately helpful. Another contribution from university science and technology comes from Sir Frederick Crawford (1991) of Aston University on Total Quality Management, presented in a CVCP Occasional Paper. Ellis (1993) reports his grappling with 'the sheer opacity of BS 5750' and the way he has managed to operationalize most of the 20 elements to fit university teaching. The quality documentation and records, the audits and the corrective action fit well with the requirements that the Funding Council will want when carrying out its 'assessments' and the Quality Council will want when carrying out 'audits'.

What has made quality quite suddenly a vital area in HE has been the very swift development of mass, rather than elite higher education. Quality and funding mechanisms are being linked, and institutions competing with each other will need to show that the job they are doing is at least adequate; now it is commercially vital that the funding council is convinced that a satisfactory job is being done. We have yet to see real punishments or rewards resulting from good or bad assessment or audit reports but we know that they are possible.

The HEQC (1994) has produced a *Checklist for Quality Assurance Systems* covering 26 topics including the evaluation of teaching and learning, staff development and student support, progress and assessment. HEQC and HEFCE have together issued a joint statement on quality assurance in which they avow that:

> Both audit and assessment are designed to work in partnership with, and reinforce, institutions' internal quality assurance processes and efforts. To assist with this objective, both audit and assessment have institutional self-assessment as a central element in their processes (HEQC/HEFCE, 1994).

Universities and colleges have been busy producing quality assurance handbooks, appointing quality managers and quality auditors and establishing academic standards units. Chapter 15 reports an exercise carried out in one department with the support of the college's Academic Standards Unit. The focus is upon student feedback, though this is only one part of course evaluation. Stringer and Finlay (1993) report a system established at the University of Ulster Faculty of Social and Health Sciences. Their 27-item questionnaire invites response on a five-point scale, as does the evaluation questionnaire used at Canterbury Christ Church College. It is interesting reviewing the different styles of questionnaire used, and to note that it usually is a questionnaire – large numbers and quantitative results have an attraction that is at times quite worrying! The University of Central England's Student Satisfaction Research Unit surveys the whole of the students' experience and uses a seven-point scale (SSRU, 1993) while the University of Central Lancashire uses a four-point scale in measuring student satisfaction.

Student evaluations have been criticized, and quite rightly so, since, though students may be considered *the customer* they are not the only customer to be served by the institution's teaching. Whatmough, in Chapter 10, has some sympathy with this view with his sixth formers, albeit in a 'listening school'. Professor Howarth (1993a) of Nottingham University claims that many of the quality assurance procedures being urged on universities by government bodies are likely to be counter-productive. He sent his article to every vice-chancellor and in the covering letter (Howarth, 1993b) wrote that:

> There is evidence in education and elsewhere that practices based on a different philosophy can be more effective. These include:

i   Giving more responsibility to students.
ii Refusing to 'spoon feed' and insisting that students search for the information they need.
iii Encouraging students to teach each other.
iv Not paying too much attention to students' evaluation of courses.

Student satisfaction surveys carried out efficiently provide useful information to feed into the decision-making system alongside other data on the quality of learning. That is what Chapter 15 suggests.

Chapters 16 and 17 describe two institution-wide systems. They are fairly expensive or, at least, have had considerable investment put in them. De Montfort, as befits a 'new' university with experience of the powerful processes of the now displaced CNAA (Council for National Academic Awards), has a structured system that revolves around a 'Course log'. This is a system still under development. Southampton's approach is based upon departmental self-assessment. Care is being taken here, in the management of a four/five year cycle of review, to ensure that both in the timing and in the content of the review, the university's system parallels that of the Funding Council. It is tricky trying to establish control and ownership of the scheme locally while conforming to a national framework.

From infant schools to universities there is evidence that none can ignore the national agencies set up to check on quality in the institution.

Satisfying the Customers

In primary education, where teachers remain for the most part with one group of up to 35 pupils, the quality focuses are specific and two of the chapters here describe initiatives directed at parents as customers in a very real sense.

The questionnaires used by Buckley (Chapter 5) and Cannon (Chapter 6) are both of interest yet it is the use to which the findings are put that is more notable. Chapter 15 does not report much on the action planning where it is the learners who are taken as the customers. Harris in Chapter 9 and Whatmough in Chapter 10 have ways of gaining the learners' views and of using them to formulate improvements. The problem of what to do when learners name teachers of whom they are critical (Whatmough, Chapter 10) will remain until we get tough enough to accept that if that is where the dissatisfaction lies, it has to be addressed. It is best if the 'customers' can focus upon the service rather than the person.

Customer orientation is vital if a quality service is to be delivered.

We need to know what they think of the service. We do not have to respond simplistically to student views, nor should we interpret 'customers' too narrowly. There are many stake-holders in the education business, many who have a concern that young (and not-so young) learners are appropriately educated. We should perhaps remember Juran's (1989) conception of the customer as being anyone upon whom the service impacts!

Tools and Instruments

One of the benefits the authors hope will stem from this book is that others will be able to borrow from and adapt the techniques and instruments which they have described. The questionnaires used by a number of the authors can be used in other circumstances. Ishikawa's fishbone technique and force field analysis have been used to good effect, though Barras (Chapter 8) is unlikely to use the former in preference to brainstorming, however it is disguised. More important than the way data are gathered is the treatment given to the data and the smooth flow from finding out to planning to do something about it. If this collection succeeds in promoting understanding of quality assurance as a social and managerial endeavour as well as a technical one it will have done its job.

Conclusion

Many of the chapters in this book record movements into the quality field and many would admit that there is some way to go to establish systems that are actually embedded in the institution's functioning. To conclude the chapter I would like to suggest that good quality assurance management systems, towards which we are working, have the following characteristics:

- they are manageable, require little time and demand resources only to the extent that they give a pay-off in return;
- they have a utility, both practical and affective, to inside audiences;
- they have a credibility to outside audiences;
- they focus on outcomes;
- they are managed courteously.

Chapter 3
TQM Goes to School

John Chesterton

The past decade has seen a phenomenal wave of interest in the application of quality management and its accompanying assortment of accreditations, methods and philosophies. Driven primarily by the West's frantic need to emulate the Far East's growing economic power, quality has been seen as the magic potion capable of restoring international competitiveness. The government has also adopted the 'mantle' with the publication of customer charters for public services, the word 'quality' itself taking on as many meanings and interpretations as any abstract word possibly can. Education has not been excluded from the quality explosion: conferences, workshops, courses and consultants abound with translations of how quality can be applied in an educational environment. Usually quality is sold under one of many brand names (BS 5750, Total Quality Management, Investors In People) causing misunderstandings as to which approach is the right one for each school. Off these, Total Quality Management (TQM) is probably the most misunderstood as it encompasses all other elements.

TQM is in many ways the application of common sense but as has been observed, sense is not that common. Simply put, it is good management practice. TQM is a philosophy that seeks to create an ethos of continuous improvement in a supportive environment where individuals take responsibility for their own processes. They are encouraged to measure their own processes without fear of blame. Underpinning these concepts are the twin themes of communication and training; communication of the school's purpose, policies and strategies; training personnel in order for them to be able to operate in the quality environment with the skills required to meet the school's objectives.

The translation of these concepts into practical management initiatives is where problems start to arise. First the use of the word 'total': as you would expect total means the whole school – senior management, staff, support staff and governors – all are expected to undertake the requirements of TQM. This poses problems for some schools where the new relationships brought about by statute have not yet fully developed. Governing bodies have yet to take on the active supportive roles required to implement TQM. However, industy/commerce-based governors who have experienced TQM implementation in their own organizations can bring valuable understanding and support to the school. Further examples of misconstruing the word 'total' are regularly seen between the senior management team and the staff: the classic launch of a quality initiative, the passing on to the staff of the quality mantle and the creation of the management myth that we've done our bit. From the staff's point of view this is seen as yet another responsibility to pile on top of all the others; without visible support, leadership and commitment, the initiative becomes another Aunt Sally for the acerbic tongues of the staffroom dinosaurs. So the first rule of implementing effectively is to think totally: how all elements of the school function to meet the purpose of the school. The key elements of TQM can be allocated under the following headings:

Customers
Processes
People
Culture.

Customers

One of the greatest disjunctures between industry and commerce and the education sector is the language used in relation to quality. The word 'customer' is the most emotive. It seems easier for the manufacturer or retailer to provide products and services to a 'customer' than a teacher in a classroom. However, the pupil is a recipient of a process and as such can be seen as a customer. There are of course differences: the pupil may not wish to receive the service and he/she may not understand exactly what their requirements are. One way to avoid this distraction is to use the language that is acceptable in your own school, so long as there is general understanding of its meaning.

The customer is the key focus of your organization, the reason for your existence, and processes are geared to satisfy their needs. To this end there is a need to review the processes that interface with the customer with due consideration given to their effectiveness.

Processes

The school's function can be broken down into processes and individuals too have their own processes, i.e., a lesson, report writing, etc. There are also key 'macro' processes which are the responsibility of senior management but are used by everyone in the school: registration; parents' evenings; sports day; examinations; professional development. The objective is to develop a culture within the school where all processes are understood by all colleagues and are reviewed as to their effectiveness. There is also the need for an objective view to be taken of such processes using the technique of 'benchmarking'. In practice schools' networks are used as a channel of ideas but with the competitive nature of education now growing, a more formalized approach is required.

Another factor to consider in reviewing the processes within the school is their relevance in a quickly changing external environment. An example of this is the rapidly changing legislation emanating from central government. The schools' ability to take on these changes is indicative of the effectiveness of their processes.

People

Education has tremendous advantages over many organizations in terms of the quality of the work force in schools. The problem is how to encourage this resource into focusing on what may be considered by them as trivial and bureaucratic. This is where the importance of communication and training become apparent. The individual needs to know the direction and aims of the school and how the processes that they operate are essential to those aims. They will also require training in order to be able to take on the control and improvement of those processes. The personnel who come into the school through the selection processes need to reflect the values and skills that meet these requirements.

Culture

For people to take ownership of their processes, to understand the direction of the school and how each individual's contribution is important, a supportive and motivating environment is needed. To create this 'culture' requires an understanding of the total quality improvement process followed by the commitment and leadership to bring about the necessary changes. Headteachers fall into the trap of identifying elements of TQM that they have implemented and hold these up as evidence of their commitment. This bypasses the first step which is the objective review of the whole organization, the standing back to consider all the strengths and weaknesses, both internal and external, of the school. From this position the path towards the construction of a TQM culture begins. The commitment of senior management to the development of this culture does not have a time limit: it has to be a permanent part of the school's culture. It has to be visible and it has to be consistent across all activities. Without this, staff will not believe in the senior management's commitment to it. Too often schools and colleges have launched TQM to the sound of trumpets and cymbals (and symbols). The first example of non-commitment to the newly-voiced proclamation denigrates the whole package, especially if there is resistance within the school or college to change. It is worthwhile considering the approach to implementation and introduction of TQM within your own culture. One way is to abandon the 'launch' approach altogether and gradually introduce the change in culture through personal example, changes in policy and practice and staff selection over a period of time.

Brand Names – BS 5750 and Investors in People (IIP)

It was stated that TQM was the umbrella that covered all elements of quality and that the other 'brand name' quality products confused the issues and understanding of TQM. From the elements of TQM described above it can be seen that BS 5750 and IIP form *part of* the TQM culture but should never be considered as the greater parts.

BS 5750

BS 5750 is a certificate that is awarded to organizations that have proven control of all their processes, including the audit and correction of those processes. It is possible to say that you may have processes that are only 50 per cent efficient but if you have them documented and they meet your specifications you will be awarded the BS 5750 certificate. The difference with TQM is that you are looking for continual improvement, i.e., 100 per cent efficiency in your processes. BS 5750 is an extremely good base to work from but in most schools and colleges the additional workload of paperwork and paperwork control causes major problems, as some colleges of FE have discovered.

IIP

Another element of TQM is the development and motivation of the people within an organization to take on the roles necessary to continually improve the processes within that organization. IIP is an accreditation awarded to organizations that have developed a structured development plan for each individual and can measure the impact of that development on the organization. Again, senior management have seen the attainment of IIP as their final goal as if it registers as the highest quality accolade; 'We're doing IIP now and given up on TQM', has been heard several times within the last year. This situation has been exacerbated by some local TECs who have promoted IIP as this year's management flavour. This approach is not helpful; yes, we need more training and skills but within a framework of understanding of organizational achievement, not just to collect the latest management badge.

Implementation of TQM

For those who have understood the scope and purpose of creating a TQM organization the next issue is one of implementation. Because of TQM's origins in industry there appears a distinct educational tendency to dismiss all possibility of its transfer to an educational environment. Issues raised include:

   language
   resources
   organization
   measurement.

Language

One of the most unfortunate aspects of TQM is the considerable amount of jargon and technical language that accompanies it. This is made worse by the assumption of practitioners that this language is universal whereas it actually has a limited public. Within education this vocabulary is a barrier to understanding and in extreme cases often offends. All terminology must be in a form that is acceptable to the educational environment.

Resources

The most frequent barrier to implementation is that education does not have unlimited resources with which to fund TQM, whereas industry and commerce are perceived as resource-rich. This is something of a fallacy; although some major companies have resourced comphrehensive training programmes with the appropriate organization to implement TQM, the vast majority have funded TQM on the back of improved efficiency and cost-savings. However, where the largest cost in educational establishments is salaries – between 60 and 90 per cent of budget – it would seem difficult to make savings without cutting staff. Yet there are opportunities to improve the efficiency of all processes within a school or college, and the area where cost savings are most likely to be made is in administration – just the same as in many industrial and commercial organizations. The greatest impact will be the effect on the standard of services provided and through this an enhanced reputation within the community and an increased demand for places. The time taken in the processes involved in implementation should be self-funding. Repeated exercises with teachers and senior management have revealed many opportunies to cut out wasted time.

Organization

Another issue that poses a considerable number of questions is that of organization. If the objective is to create a culture where individuals and teams can control their own processes and improve them to meet the organization's objectives, how are they going to do this when they are unavailable for 75 per cent of their time because they are engaged in their solitary productive work of teaching? How can the organization provide the training necessary when there is such limited time in which to do so? How is the organization going to communicate, not just day-to-day issues but the objectives and direction as well? Suggestions abound, from greater empowerment of departmental/faculty heads to a reduced senior management team with the resources saved providing an improved support system for teachers/lecturers. Allocation of one staff member to take on a coordinator's role is an expensive resource and has been used in colleges of FE to introduce initiatives such as BS 5750, but in most schools this would be considered a luxury. Only time will tell which is the best way forward as each school/college will have its own structure to provide for its own unique set of circumstances. The important point is that senior management teams, where the power actually lies, will actually consider these issues as in a lot of cases they will be forced by circumstance to take them on.

Measurement

Mention the word 'measurement' to most groups of teachers and they will say that it's not possible in education. This is not an idle generalization – in the course of tutoring on quality management over the last four years, I have heard the same comment every time, without fail. The purpose of measurement is to improve the processes measured; without measurement how do we know if the processes we operate are effective? There is a fear that measurement may reveal non-conformances and someone will have to take the blame. This highlights another aspect of the culture to be created: that measurement is positive. If things do go wrong then it is the process that is the problem not necessarily the person operating it – a culture of no blame.

Another problem with measurement is in its application to classroom processes. The point is raised that it is virtually impossible to measure the effect of a lesson or tutorial on each pupil or student as it is an abstract intangible output. The response to this is to take a few paces backwards, and measure the mechanistic processes that create the best antecedents and environment for the teaching to take place. That means having the correct teacher in the right classroom at the right time with the correct class and all the necessary materials. Once all these are in place the quality of the teaching/learning can be reviewed. There is a host of measurements that can be applied to educational processes that will highlight areas for improvement. The pity is that you don't actually have to be efficient to get by!

Myths and Legends of TQM

The biggest disadvantage that TQM has in an educational context is that it has originated from an industrial base. Within education this is viewed as industry imposing a mechanistic straitjacket on schools almost as a practical follow-up to the government's restrictive education legislation. This is totally unfounded as industry itself has yet to achieve the benefits that are possible. The CBI surveyed those companies that had commenced implementation of TQM processes and in only 20 per cent of the companies had there been measureable benefits. This does not invalidate TQM; there are many reasons for the failures, including lack of management commitment and underestimating the scope of the changes necessary and the time-scales involved. Furthermore, short-termism has always been one of Britain's negative approaches to business; TQM, however, counters this by requiring a longer-term and continuous process of review, revision and implementation.

Education has several advantages over industry in implementation. The teaching staff involved are academically well-qualified and the existence of the collegiate style of operation within educational institutions is a firm base to start from. Staff commitment to the values and objectives of the school/college tends to be higher. It is fundamental that staff take ownership of TQM principles, in order to improve their processes, and to do that they have to know the direction of the organization and support the values and the rules by which it operates. Another advantage is the size of school or college; in general they have 6–60 staff, meaning that the correct type of leadership can have an immediate impact on the culture of the school or college.

In September 1993 schools began the four-year cycle of inspection controlled by OFSTED. Although the thought of teams of inspectors burrowing through their schools seems like a nightmare for headteachers, there are advantages. At the beginning of this chapter I suggested that the starting point for implementation was a review of your organization to identify the strengths and weaknesses; OFSTED reports are exactly that. Some schools and colleges are already a long way along the path of implementation, and the OFSTED report will confirm progress. Sections of the inspection framework refer specifically to long-term planning, control of processes and leadership, all of which are integral to TQM.

TQM is too important to be dismissed for any reasons as glib as those mentioned in this chapter. The elements of TQM need to replicated in all our business and public institutions for the benefit of all, including the people that work in them.

Chapter 4
A Quest for Quality in Key Stage 1 Assessment

Ruth Hendry

Setting the Scene

The unchallenged aim of all concerned with the education of children of all ages is quality. Thus far agreement is easy; but to agree a definition of 'quality' is not a simple matter. As Edward Sallis (1993) points out:

> ...many people find quality a most enigmatic concept. It is perplexing to define and even more difficult to measure. One person's idea of quality often conflicts with another's and as we are all too aware, no two experts ever come to the same conclusion when discussing what makes a good school or college.

In these times of market forces in education, quality becomes doubly important, for it takes on not only a philosophical context but also an economic one:

> Quality is what makes the difference between things being excellent or run-of-the-mill. Increasingly in education quality makes the difference between success and failure.

In my own school, where I am a Year 2 class teacher, we have an even greater than usual onus on us to provide and prove quality in our education, since the physical conditions under which we work present probably the worst-case scenario imaginable for the education of Key Stage 1 children. The school is an infants' school serving the centre of Ramsgate, an unemployment 'blackspot' with a high proportion of one-parent families.

The school building is Victorian, consisting of three classrooms and a very small hall. For several years, due to pressure of numbers, it has been necessary for the school to accommodate five classes of children, which means that two classes – the two Year 2 classes –

daily have to make two journeys to and from temporary accommodation situated a quarter of a mile away from the main buildings. The classrooms are situated up a flight of stone steps, the only toilet facilities being a mobile block outside. Until very recently there was no water in the classrooms and buckets of water had to be carried up and down stairs daily.

The management implications of working in these physical circumstances are complex for all concerned, but particularly for myself and the deputy head whose classrooms are located at such a distance from the main school. Not the least of these problems is that we lose something in the region of five hours teaching time per week due to our constant perambulations.

In these days of supposed parental choice, if we are not delivering what parents perceive to be a 'quality' education to their children, their right is to remove them to another school. There is nothing in our physical conditions to either attract or keep pupils. However, possible help is at hand. Surely every headteacher in the country will identify with this comment by Edgar Willie (1992), regarding business management:

> ...the purpose of work is to provide customers with something that will delight them and make them want to keep paying your salary, by buying the product or service you provide.

Can we, in education, learn something from business and industry in our search for quality? Many people express doubts. How can the language of business management be translated to the educational context without the depersonalization of the child? The aim in industry is for conformity; the aim in education is emphatically *not* the cloning of human beings. However, Willie says:

> The total quality approach is about people and attitudes. It's not about techniques and procedures as such. It includes them, and it needs them. However, it's people who actually use them.

This being so, then perhaps TQM does have something to offer us in schools. The TQM approach to management stresses the importance of relationships, of quality as all-pervading, an ethos, a culture. It is not something which can be achieved overnight – indeed it is not something which has an ultimate end product, since the TQM creed is based on the philosophy of continuous improvement:

> If culture is the personality of an organisation, then a quality school is restless, constantly questioning, never satisfied, challenging norms and believing that things can always be better. Quality management requires

a belief in an infinite capacity for improvement of organisations, processes and people (West-Burnham, 1992).

The Project

The idea of striving for total quality is one which has proved very attractive to the headteacher and staff alike. The establishment of a total quality ethos is an incremental process and, as a starting point and something of an experiment, it was agreed by the headteacher that I could take responsibility for managing a review of assessment procedures through Key Stage 1, using a total quality approach and appropriate techniques.

We decided to begin with assessment procedures in response to a plea from myself and the other Year 2 teacher that teacher assessment and recording in a more formal way could be more evenly spread across the Key Stage, to alleviate the burden on Year 2 teachers at the end of the Stage.

In the Spring and Summer terms of 1993 we felt that we were lurching from one crisis to another as we struggled to cope with Standard Assessment Tasks (SATs) which were in themselves very time-consuming to administer to a class of 30 children in any meaningful way, and at the same time trying to make fair and valid judgements about the other Statements of Attainment in maths, English and science. In addition, all Statements of Attainment in history, geography and technology had to be statutorily assessed and reported in 1993 – something in the region of 2,000 separate assessments to be made!

We were also concerned to see our teaching becoming assessment-led, as we desperately tried to cover all the Attainment Targets in order that we could then assess them! This, from Sue Pidgeon, describing the Spring of 1991, strikes a real chord of recognition:

> Good early years practice was quickly replaced by an assessment-led curriculum. In many classes children were ricocheting from one unrelated activity to another to ensure all attainment targets were covered: there was no time for children to learn in any meaningful way, things were just 'taught' in ways far removed from good practice (Pidgeon, 1992).

This was crisis management at its worst, and must surely have been detracting from quality. Something had to be done!

We began our review on a School INSET day. I introduced the problem in hand and attempted, with other staff, to produce a set of aims. Teamwork is a very important aspect of TQM; every member of the establishment is regarded as a vital member of the team. I was anxious at this stage to present the project as equally relevant to all members of staff and to ensure that they all felt they had an important contribution to make: 'one of the keys to quality is to empower and encourage people to give input from their knowledge and experience' (Willie, 1992).

Another of my main concerns during this initial session was to emphasize the positive aspects of what was already being done in the Year 1 classes, to prevent a further decline in morale at this stage of a long and fraught school year, and to attempt to convince other staff that investment in planning now would actually mean less work in the future.

The staff were all very cooperative and happy to share their own viewpoints, although there were reservations from one Year 1 teacher about the amount of time that she would be required to spend on assessment rather than teaching. However, by the end of the session we had arrived at a series of aims for the project:

- to produce a system of assessment for Key Stage 1 which accurately reflects the child's progress in the National Curriculum;
- it must be valid, reliable, standardized, objective, manageable to carry out and record, and easily accessible:
- it must be an effective tool in the teaching/assessment/planning cycle and be able to identify individual children's strengths and weaknesses.

TQM advocates the theory that all work is a process, that in every process there are a number of suppliers and clients, and that the needs of all of these must be adequately met. Therefore in every process undertaken in school the needs of the parents, the children, the government, the LEA and the teacher must be met.

In the light of this philosophy of 'delighting the customer' I next, in consultation with the headteacher, produced an Output Needs Analysis worksheet for the work process of KS1 assessment. We identified eight customers and their needs from the assessment process:

| The child | An appropriately planned learning environment. Special Educational Needs identified as they occur. Positive feedback. |
| Parents | Knowledge of the child's progress compared to other children of a similar age. Awareness of problems as they occur. |

Teachers	Knowledge of the child's learning ability and progress. Comparison to age-related abilities. Information for planning. Feedback for effective teaching – or otherwise!
Headteacher	Knowledge of teacher effectiveness. Knowledge to inform decisions regarding organization of activities and curriculum. Comparison with other schools and across the school. To satisfy parents – public relations. To satisfy the LEA and OFSTED.
Governors	Reassurance that their ultimate responsibility in law for curriculum effectiveness and effective use of budget is being fulfilled.
Local Education Authority	Information to ensure a cohesive approach across the authority.
Government	Political needs – to raise standards and gain votes. Accountability to the electorate.
Society	A continuous supply of well-educated people.

In the face of this daunting list of customers and their needs, in our next staff meeting I decided to look at the criteria set out in the new OFSTED (1993) handbook for measuring the quality of assessment. How would we measure up to their standards? To this end I devised a questionnaire to be answered by discussion and agreement, based on the OFSTED criteria. This, we hoped, would show us where our short-comings in assessment lay. The results were as follows:

YES (✓), NO (X) OR (?)

Is there a coherent assessment policy? **X**

Is it adhered to? **X**

Are assessments accurate? **?**

Are assessments used to help individual pupils make progress? **✓**

Are assessment criteria clear? **X**

Is there evidence of planning in response to assessment? **✓**

Is assessment moderated? **X**

Is the quality of marking consistent? **X**

Do records and reports match legal requirements? **✓**

Are records clear, systematic, manageable, consistent and useful? **✓**

Do records inform planning? **✓**

From this it was immediately evident that our recording system is adequate, but that, although assessment takes place, it is neither standardized nor moderated. We all make assessments but we have no means at present of ensuring that our judgements are the same as those of our colleagues. The agreed action required was to review the Whole School Assessment Policy, ensure that all staff are aware of its content and ensure that it is adhered to. We also agreed that a marking policy is needed.

Assessment procedures need to be agreed throughout the school and assessments need to be moderated by agreement trialling. We therefore agreed, as a long-term project, to develop a bank of standardized assessment tasks to be used throughout the Key Stage as evidence of National Curriculum attainment. There will be at least one task for each level up to Level 3 of each Attainment Target in the core subjects. These will be trialled to ensure that they accurately reflect attainment of the concept required at the correct level.

As an off-shoot of this process, we hope to make the keeping of evidence of attainment much more straightforward. A School Portfolio will be produced, including examples of children's performances in the tasks. We will then be able to say, 'When we speak about a child having attained Level 2 at AT1 Maths, this is what we mean'. We hope that this will relieve the necessity for keeping large amounts of evidence for each child and will make our record keeping more meaningful.

We then tried to identify which areas of the curriculum presented us with the most problems in the area of assessment. It was agreed that Attainment Target 1 in both maths and science were the most difficult to assess. These require children to hypothesize, investigate, problem solve, experiment and explore, and are thus not easily 'tested'. We carried out one of the TQM problem-solving exercises to attempt to analyse which were the major causes of this problem. We utilized 'Ishikawa's Fishbone' technique, one of the techniques advocated by Kaoru Ishikawa, a leading Japanese exponent of TQM. This tool is used when an institution or team needs to identify and explore the possible causes of a problem or look for the factors which affect the quality of a process, usually in four categories. It is often drawn on a diagram resembling a fishbone. The results are shown in Figure 4.1. (See Vorley, 1991, and Murgatroyd and Morgan, 1993, for further examples of this technique.) It was then possible to agree on the two which cause the greatest problems: insufficient human resources and equipment, and insufficient time. Under present conditions it is impossible to provide greater human

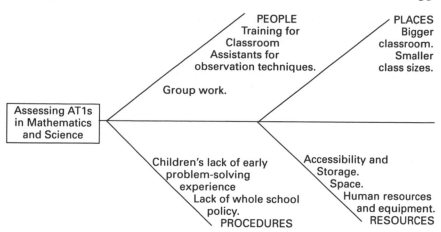

Figure 4.1 Ishikawa's Fishbone

resources or time, but it is my intention as a result of these findings to carry out analyses of both time and resource management in the classroom.

Our next concern relating to the assessment process was to define our measurements of quality. What are our performance indicators which will help us to measure the effectiveness of our procedures? We arrived at nine possible indicators of quality:

Are parents and the LEA satisfied?
Are the results usually what we would expect? If not, are the assessment procedures valid?
Is the child making progress?
Are the child's problems being identified? Diagnosed? Addressed?
Are the parents aware of the child's progress?
Are the parents aware of the child's problems?
Are the teachers' planning processes effective and appropriate?
Are standards generally uniform across the school?
Are standards being raised?

Our current feeling is that if we can answer yes to all of these questions, our assessment procedures are effective.

This is the stage at which the project was left at the end of the last academic year. Since then we have begun discussion of formulating assessment tasks for maths and science Attainment Target 1. Debate has been lively (!) particularly in two areas. The first area of difficulty in reaching agreement is that of the starting point for designing the tasks. The more experienced members of staff feel that we should look at activities already taking place in the classroom and use these as the basis for assessment procedures. The major problem with this is that of uniformity – we all approach the attainment targets through different activities and this would make standardization and moderation more difficult and time-consuming. The less experienced members of staff would feel more comfortable taking the Statement of Attainment as the starting point and designing a task which would show an understanding of the Statement if successfully completed. The debate continues.

The second area of discussion is perhaps even more difficult to reach agreement on. By the very nature of National Curriculum Statements of Attainment, assessment of these must be summative. However, we feel that formative assessment is often most useful from a diagnostic and planning point of view. The Task Group on Assessment and Testing (TGAT) Report (DES, 1988, para.23) reinforces our opinions, setting out several purposes that the data produced by National Curriculum assessment should be capable of fulfilling:

> *Formative* – so that the positive achievements of a pupil may be recognized and discussed and the appropriate next steps may be planned.
> *Diagnostic* – through which learning difficulties may be scrutinized and classified so that appropriate remedial help and guidance can be provided.
> *Summative* – for the recording of the overall achievement of a pupil in a systematic way.
> *Evaluative* – by means of which some aspects of the work of a school, an LEA or other discrete part of the educational service can be assessed and/or reported upon.

These purposes seem to bear more than a passing resemblance to our agreed performance indicators of quality, but little resemblance to the actual outcomes of National Curriculum assessment. Others have obviously faced this dilemma before:

> ...formative and summative assessment cannot easily draw on the same information because their needs are very different and, where there is a conflict, it will always be the needs of summative and evaluative assessment that prevail (Barrs, 1990).

It seems an almost insoluble problem: attempting to maintain formative assessment as part of good early years practice and yet also trying to carry out our statutory responsibility to assess children's progress through the National Curriculum in a meaningful way.

Update

The Dearing Report (SCAA, 1994) has caused us to put the brakes on our project somewhat for various reasons, the main one being that, after the 1995 KS1 assessment procedure is completed, we will be presented with a totally revised National Curriculum, with who knows what to be assessed – and who knows how! However, production of the School Portfolio is proceeding, and in fact is now being advocated for all primary schools by the Kent Curriculum Services Agency.

The School Assessment and Recording Policy has been revised and will be used as a guide of and to good practice in the school. We also are very much aware of the work still to be done to see us through the inevitable visit from OFSTED.

Stop press: Even as I write, the first turf is being turned for the building of our brand new, purpose-built school. From Quality in a slum to Quality in a palace!

Conclusion

We all feel that we have broadened our understanding of KS1 assessment by taking a TQM approach. It has forced us to look much further afield then previously in our consideration of needs in the assessment process, and our aim in our quest for quality and continuous improvement is that every child in our care will benefit from a more tightly organized and monitored establishment.

One aspect of TQM which has caused us problems in this context is the notion of zero defects. This is attainable in industry since raw materials can be inspected for quality and any sub-standard material discarded; also, inanimate materials are predictable. However, when children are the raw materials for your processes the unpredictability factor makes the quest for zero defects much more difficult, no matter how watertight you feel your procedures are.

Having said this, it must be acknowledged that, to have a quality culture and ethos in any school is to be desired. To have procedures which set out aims and then check whether they are being met and whether the results are as expected must improve efficiency. Above all, to have procedures in place which automatically come into operation when a problem occurs must be the best way to avoid what so many of us – whether we are headteachers, heads of department or class teachers – are guilty of today: *crisis management*. How wonderful to ultimately be able to eliminate that enemy of quality!

Chapter 5
Parents in Partnership

Kevin Buckley

Serving the Customer

A quality organization, according to West-Burnham (1992), exists to
meet its customer's needs. It appears, therefore, that in order to
achieve 'quality' an organization needs to identify its customers.
West-Burnham stresses that a customer is anyone to whom a product
or service is provided and that there are internal and external
customers. In the case of a school the customers can include children, parents, governors, inspectors, politicians, the LEA, local
employers and members of the local community. In order to provide
satisfaction, the needs of the customer must be defined, specific
actions should be taken to satisfy those needs, complaints and
concerns should be welcomed, and various techniques should be
used to find out about customer satisfaction. In short, the school
needs to develop a partnership with its customers and partnership
activity should be promoted in pursuit of school improvement policies (Henley, 1987). This school, as part of its development plan,
decided to do just that.

Parents as Customers

There are a number of very good reasons, both within and outside
the quality debate, as to why schools should develop a partnership
with parents. Not only do the 1944 and 1988 Education Acts
promote the notion of teachers and parents working jointly in children's education but greater parental involvement may enhance the
child's progress at school. Lopate *et. al.* (1969) state that increased
achievement may be due to the lessening of distance between the
goals of the home and the goals of the school. Everard and Morris
(1990) talk of 'fruitful relationships' (p.223) whereby problems are
jointly resolved by home and school, and of 'reservoirs of talent and

goodwill' among parents waiting to be tapped. Perhaps the most beneficial result of greater involvement is increased confidence, in parents who feel that they have a role to play in the decision-making process, and in children who feel an increased sense of control through knowing that their parents are more involved.

With the introduction of open enrolment, it is necessary, for survival purposes, to be as attractive as possible to parents in order to maintain or increase the roll number.

Quality Circles

According to the DTI (1992b), a quality circle is an essential part of Total Quality Management and one of the most effective forms of teamwork. Robson (1988), West-Burnham (1992) and the DTI all give similar definitions of quality circles, the key characteristics of which are:

- a group of between three and twelve members;
- all volunteers;
- from the same work area;
- meeting regularly, perhaps once a week for an hour;
- led by a supervisor;
- identifying, analysing and solving work-related problems;
- recommending solutions to management;
- implementing solutions.

There are five features inherent in a successful quality circle:

- everybody in the organization needs to be aware of the existence, use and structure of a quality circle;
- attendance must be voluntary;
- quality circles should be unbureaucratic;
- they should not become pressure groups;
- they should be backed by the management.

A major benefit of quality circles is the improvement in two-way communication. Management becomes more conscious of the problems of the staff, through the circle activities, whilst staff become more aware of the difficulties of management.

There are, however, reasons why a quality circle may fail. Robson (1988) warns that the way in which it is introduced may cause its demise. If it is seen to be a management gimmick then that is exactly what it will become, and it will not last. Likewise, if it is introduced and treated in a simplistic manner, it will not be taken seriously for long.

The Quality Street Gang!

In my organization, it was decided that a quality circle approach would be the most appropriate for developing the theme of a partnership with parents. A quality circle of four members was formed.

An early concern was that these members would feel anxiety as they had 'put their heads on the block' by volunteering. Robson (1988) warns that there are likely to be colleagues who will be unconvinced of the utility of the strategy and that the circle members may feel out on a limb. Indeed there were some jokes about 'magic circles' although the quality circle members did become affectionately known as 'the quality street gang'!

The Quality Circle at Work

It was suggested at the initial meeting of the quality circle to adopt Robson's (1988, p.76) ten-step framework for success:

1. brainstorm the list of problems;
2. select the general theme out of this list;
3. analyse the problem which has been selected;
4. decide what facts are needed to be able to solve the problem;
5. gather data about the problem;
6. interpret the data collected;
7. devise a solution to the problem based on facts;
8. prepare and give a presentation of the solution to the management;
9. implement the solution if agreed by management;
10. monitor the results of the solution.

The first two steps were very straightforward. As the circle had been formed for the purpose of tackling one particular issue, although other issues may have been tackled at a later date, step 1 was unnecessary and step 2 irrelevant. Step 3, an analysis of the problem, involved discussion of the background to the problem, how it came to light, and why it was necessary to solve the problem. Additionally, it was suggested that an audit of the situation be taken in order to gain a clear picture of the problem. The following audit sheet was devised with the quality circle's responses underlined:

Parents are kept informed of all developments in the school
curriculum.   Yes   <u>?</u>   No

Parents are encouraged to visit classrooms and corridors.
                                                    Yes   ?   <u>No</u>

Parent evenings are well organized.   Yes   <u>?</u>   No

Maximum use is made of parental skills in classrooms.
                                                    Yes   <u>?</u>   No

The school gives the impression of being welcoming to parents.
                                                    Yes   <u>?</u>   No

Parents are kept clearly informed of their child's progress.
                                                    Yes   <u>?</u>   No

Newsletters are not 'moan' sheets.   Yes   <u>?</u>   No

Parents are aware of the purpose and function of the governing
body.   Yes   ?   <u>No</u>

Parents know the role of each teacher.   <u>Yes</u>   ?   No

Parents are encouraged to help with their child's work at home.
                                                    Yes   <u>?</u>   No

Step 4 is to decide what facts are needed. The analysis and the audit
had both provided the quality circle with many facts to help in
addressing the challenges, but it was suggested that the 'pros and
cons' of developing a partnership with parents should be considered.
Thus, steps 5 and 6, gathering and interpreting data, became an exercise in Lewin's (1947) 'force-field' analysis in which the driving and
restraining forces likely to affect a proposed change are identified.
The analysis resulting from this is set out in Figure 5.1.

The strongest driving forces were identified as the school's roll,
the financial position and improved discipline. A drop in the school's
roll would possibly mean a reduction in the staffing level as well as
reduced finances. The financial position, however, could, through a
greater involvement by parents, be enhanced both by maintaining the
school's roll and by having more fund-raising activities. As far as
discipline is concerned, it was felt that many teachers would like

Figure 5.1 Force-field analysis

parents to be aware of the sanctions that existed.

The strongest restraining forces were identified as the strain on teachers' time and weakened security. Time was very much a concern but the argument against greater parental involvement could be challenged by suggesting that, in the long term, such involvement could help reduce the teachers' workload. Security could be taken as a separate issue.

Some of the restraining forces could be turned around and made into driving forces. If parents have misconceptions based on their own school experiences, then more openness on the part of the school would help to drive out fear, mistrust or even dislike of their child's school. The concern about parental help being detrimental could also be turned around. Some parents would attempt to help their children, rightly so, whether they were given guidance or not. Therefore, better communication between school and parent would be likely to reduce the possibility of detrimental assistance.

Dauber and Epstein (1989), in their comparitive study focusing on parents' attitudes and activities, found that most parents wanted schools to advise them on how to help their own children at home; that parents believed schools needed to strengthen activities giving parents specific information on academic subjects; that parents who had received guidance from schools on how to help at home spent more time doing so; and that the level of parents' involvement is directly linked to the specific practices of the school that encourage involvement.

Step 7 is to devise a solution based on the facts. The quality circle drew up the following list of target areas, each of which could be developed to improve the partnership with parents:

- conversation with parents;
- consultation evenings;
- reports;
- newsletters;
- curriculum workshops;
- relationship with parent governors;
- homework policy;
- paired/shared reading;
- fund-raising;
- parent helpers;
- discipline;
- school prospectus;
- crisis management.

Of these, curriculum workshops, consultation evenings and reports were prioritized for the first term because they all would occur during the term anyway; the newsletters were included after it was suggested that they were becoming 'moansheets'! Thus, as Step 8, an action plan was drawn up by the quality circle to make improvements in these areas.

The Curriculum Meeting

Step 9 is to implement the solution if agreed by the management. As this was so, work began on attaining the first target – a curriculum meeting for parents. Sullivan (1991) suggests the following format for the organization of such a meeting:

purpose;
planning;
timing;
publicity;
displays;
presentation;
activities and equipment;
closing the workshop;
evaluation.

Geography, and its cross-curricular implications was identified as the subject which most needed to be defined to the parents. The subject coordinator took on the responsibility for planning and it was deemed essential that all staff clearly understood the purpose of the meeting. The evening least likely to clash with popular television viewing was chosen and details of the meeting were sent, well in advance, to the parents. Posters advertising the event were strategically placed.

Displays of geography work from all year groups were set up. A guest speaker from the LEA curriculum support agency was invited and brought many resources. The school displayed its own resources with which parents were encouraged to familiarize themselves. At the end of the evening there was a plenary session for parents to ask formal questions followed by an opportunity for parents to talk informally with the available teachers.

Step 10 is to monitor the results of the solution. The meeting was attended by approximately 40 parents representing a roll of 420 children. Whilst a greater turnout would have been appreciated, this was an improvement on the previous meeting's attendance of just under 30. If deemed successful, this would possibly lead to greater attendances in future. An evaluation sheet, containing a note of thanks and a brief explanation of its purposes, was issued to each parent. The sheet contained five questions:

1. Did you find the evening generally helpful?

Yes   Unsure   No

2. Did you find the evening informative, i.e., did you learn about new National Curriculum developments?

Yes   Unsure   No

3. Did you find the evening a practical help, i.e., did you learn of ways you can develop practical points at home or out on excursions?   Yes   Unsure   No

4. Was the evening a pleasant social occasion?

Yes   Unsure   No

5. Would you like to make any further comments?

Sixteen parents took the time to complete the sheets, all of whom answered 'yes' to questions 1 and 3, indicating that the evening was helpful, both theoretically and practically. Thirteen parents found the evening informative with the remaining three being 'unsure'. Two parents were unsure about the evening being a 'pleasant social occasion', the rest answered 'yes'. Six parents made additional comments; mainly these were words of appreciation although two parents took the opportunity to criticize those parents who did not attend. One parent suggested more practical experiences, which was considered in the planning of future curriculum evenings. Generally, therefore, the quality of the responses indicated the evening was successful.

Consultation Evenings

It is vital that parents are given the opportunity to discuss their child's progress with the school. It is possible that the ways in which such consultations are organized might lead to dissatisfaction from parents and that they might gain an inaccurate picture of their child's attainment. The circle was able to identify the main criticism voiced by parents who had attended previous evenings – the waiting! The solution to this problem appeared to be two-fold: avoid delays; make any delays more comfortable.

It transpired that a number of parents had been left waiting for considerable periods of time despite being punctual for their appointment. Such delays can be very frustrating. It was proposed that teachers should limit each appointment to ten minutes duration. Parents would be informed of this in the letter of invitation but given the opportunity to make a further appointment if they felt it necessary. It was also suggested that teachers keep a check-list of the important issues to be covered at each consultation so as to keep to the matters in hand. Sometimes delays had occurred because parents were late for their appointments. In order to avoid this parents were offered a choice of time blocks before being allocated a set time. Parents were also requested to list their other children, if any, who attended the school. Teachers could then liaise so that no parents were given times which 'clashed' and so that they had time to travel from one teacher to the next.

The quality circle was concerned that, when waiting occurred, the parents should be kept as comfortable as possible. Ensuring there were sufficient seats was the obvious first step. It was also suggested that as many different children as possible had their work displayed so that parents could see their own child's efforts, that videos of children working be shown and soft music should be played. This also prevented parents from accidentally overhearing teachers' confidential conversations with other parents in the more open parts of the school.

Approximately 90 per cent of all parents attended a consultation making it very successful in those terms. The majority of the remaining 10 per cent who did not attend were parents of Year 6 pupils who presumably felt that, as their children were leaving, there was little more that could be done. Many parents commented on the effective time-keeping of teachers and there were very few delays during the evenings. The displays were praised and the seating arrangements for waiting parents were appreciated even though a heavy storm meant that some hasty rearranging of seats took place for those parents waiting outside mobile classrooms!

Reports

The main problem which the quality circle encountered when considering reports to parents on children's progress was that the legal requirements are very prescriptive. The DfE (1992a) clearly outlines these as being 'brief particulars' of subjects studied, details of pupil's general progress, details of arrangements for discussing the reports, a summary of the pupil's attendance record, results of assessments and, at the end of each Key Stage, the pupil's National Curriculum level. Thus, the quality circle concerned itself less with the report format and more with the presentation and content of the report.

After considering a number of draft versions, each of which moved away from the more traditional report 'sheet', the staff decided on an aesthetically pleasing report in booklet form. This report contained adequate space for comments on each of the subjects but in proportion, i.e. the 'core' subjects were given more space than the other foundation subjects, and it satisfied all the legal requirements.

Concern was expressed that the overall presentation of a report would be meaningless if the report was not completed satisfactorily. Therefore, a staff development session was devoted to discussion about the quality of the reporting and good or bad practice. The result of this was that a 'dummy' report was produced which could be considered as a reasonable example. Every member of staff was also issued with a 'phrase bank' to assist when difficulty in expressing a particular issue was encountered. However, it was pointed out that over-use of such a bank would result in reports being too similar, and it was stressed that the bank was for assistance only.

No negative comments were received from parents about the new format. There was, however, feedback from staff, a number of whom complained that the report writing was too time-consuming. The quality circle, accordingly, made this concern a priority issue for future meetings.

Newsletters

The quality circle produced suggestions for the improvement of newsletters under four headings:

    regularity;
    presentation;
    content;
    distribution.

It was decided to limit newsletters to one a month except when an urgent issue arose. There would be a difference in colour between news sheets and formal letters, and a quality word-processing package would be sought. 'Moans' would be limited and more information, explanation and gratitude would be included. Some wider educational issues might also be covered. Distribution would continue to be through the children but with copies displayed around the school. A numbering system would also be introduced.

Time worked against the quality circle and so did limited resources, especially different coloured paper! Thus, these plans were temporarily shelved.

Satisfied Customers and an end to Mid-career Crises!

Although there was still some way to go before the organization could consider itself to be a TQM establishment, the steps it took in that direction were all positive. The question of customer satisfaction had been debated at great length and many plans had been put into practice. The staff, who had always appreciated their accountability, seemed to be relieved that action was being taken to provide the school and its customers with a system of quality assurance.

Finally, it is useful to consider the views of one particular member of the quality circle in mid-career who, through quality circle activities, began to feel happier in all aspects of his work. He explained that he felt valued for the first time in a long while and that he was empowered by the feeling of ownership of the policies which were being implemented. West-Burnham (1992) emphasizes that 'quality can only be achieved by a valued work force' (p.26). The quality circle approach has served to satisfy not only our customers but ourselves too.

Chapter 6

Communication and Quality in the Primary School

Glen Cannon

The School and its Environment

Our school is one of eight primary schools in a town which is situated on the border of two Greater London boroughs. It serves a mixed social area but with a majority of families in local authority housing. There is a very high proportion of families who receive welfare support due to unemployment, single-parent status or low income. Of the eight schools, four of them have very significantly higher proportions (i.e., greater than 40 per cent by audit) of children with special educational needs (SEN). This reflects the degree of social disadvantage that exists within the catchment area of the town. In the case of our own school, the total number of children who appear on the LEA's audit for SEN amounts to 68 per cent of the total number of pupils in the school and of these, more than half have a combination of both learning difficulty and behaviour problems.

The abolition of defined catchment areas and freedom of parental choice has led to a degree of instability in the school populations as some parents exercise their right of choice by selecting a school with a lower proportion of SEN, if necessary transporting their children to schools in the surrounding villages. A significant number of parents whose children are experiencing learning or behavioural difficulties in their schools attempt to 'solve' their problems by transferring to a different school. It is not uncommon for some children to have had three or more changes of primary school by the age of 8 yet to have lived continuously at the same address since birth.

In a 'market economy' where schools depend on maintaining their number on roll, there is a real difficulty in promoting the image of a school in an area of social disadvantage and with such a high proportion of children identified as SEN. There seemed to be two major areas that needed to be investigated in our own case: the first was to be certain of the confidence of parents in the quality of the school, i.e. that we were doing a good and an effective job and particularly that the proportion of children with SEN was not a diminishing factor in the overall quality of education; the second was to be sure that the school was a welcoming and non-threatening environment in which all parents had confidence, and that they felt able to meet on friendly terms with teaching staff, working together with us in all matters relating to the education of their children.

Education and the TQM 'Gurus'

My introduction to the concepts of TQM, in relation to the field of primary school education, has revealed them as natural and with obvious application. TQM offers various models by which exactly the kinds of problems outlined might be investigated and resolved. It further offers means by which, in everyday practice, quality in every aspect is monitored and maintained.

In Parsons' description of worshipping at the temple of TQM in Chapter 1, he gives an amusing but accurate analogy of a wide range of basic religious experiences. There are fascinating parallels that indeed touch on the worlds of religious experience and expectation, including that of the 'guru'. I would add my own example to these in consideration of the work of Philip Crosby, one of the acknowledged TQM 'gurus'. I have a serious problem with the notion of setting goals of absolute perfection. In the primary school, the notion of 'zero defects' when applied to some of my delightful juniors does seem rather a remote goal (Crosby, 1979)! I feel these to be unrealistic, unattainable and likely to have a demoralizing effect in the long term. Wesley's doctrine of 'sinless perfection' certainly caused some heartache amongst sincere and well-intentioned people in his day! As well as Crosby, I considered the work of Deming (1988), Juran (1988), Feigenbaum (1983) and Ishikawa (1976) and also the 'excellence' movement, which is less industry- and product-oriented and more aware of attitude and agreed values. Deming (1988) was of particular help, in both his 14 points and four principles. It would certainly be a noble and a well-received notion if we were able to give up a dependence on inspection as a quality indicator *because we had adopted quality as a part of the product* (the third of Deming's 14 points).

Deming asserts that information, experience and a transformation of our understanding are crucial to quality. They are an important and intrinsic part of the cycle. It is not enough, he says, for everyone simply to 'do their best' for he asserts that, '*It is first necessary that people know what to do*', and that '*Long term commitment to new learning and new philosophy is required...*' (Deming,1988). There can be little dispute with these points, or indeed the four principles of his 'System of profound knowledge' which can apply to any organization irrespective of it being a manufacturing concern or a service.

At the point when we decided to embark upon a 'quality assessment' exercise, a number of significant initiatives had already been made in the school, particularly in the development of the curriculum and towards raising the ethos and image of the school. The most radical and effective change had been the evolution of a firm policy to promote good behaviour. The effect of these changes was already beginning to provoke some very positive responses from parents, governors and from the wider community. These were, however subjective and unquantifiable. They offered no basis for us to assess how effective we had been and more pertinently, *no indication of 'if' or 'where' in the eyes of our customers, we were continuing to fail.*

Quality Involves us All!

One of the first principles is the involvement of all staff in the quality concept. I introduced the concept to my senior management team who drew up with me a staff/governors audit questionnaire and my deputy, who was also chair of the pastoral and welfare sub-committee, agreed to include the matter on the agenda for that committee's inaugural meeting. Dr Kaoru Ishikawa is best known for his pioneering of 'quality circle' management (although this was developed from Deming) and for his now famous cause-and-effect diagram that is often referred to as an 'Ishikawa diagram' (Ishikawa, 1976). In particular, Ishikawa applies the principles of TQM on a much wider basis than merely to the 'product'. He includes in his company-wide philosophy the notion that quality should apply to after-sales service, quality of management, the quality of the company itself and the people who are associated with it. I find this to be a far more comfortable notion in an educational environment because it makes sense of the variety of 'product' and 'customer' definitions that apply to us. Furthermore, the functional simplicity of Ishikawa's cause-and-effect diagram seemed to us to be a very sound basis on which to conduct our internal enquiries.

I determined that I would use the fishboning technique (Ishikawa diagram), focusing on the internal and external communications of the school as a preliminary investigation amongst the staff as it met the criteria that I considered to be most appropriate, namely that (a) it involved the 'brainstorming' and involvement of a wider group of people; (b) it is a technique which focuses attention on the most urgent matters. Therefore, any resulting changes that are made are most likely to have significant and noticeable effect. Figure 6.1 shows the results of the staff 'brainstorming' session.

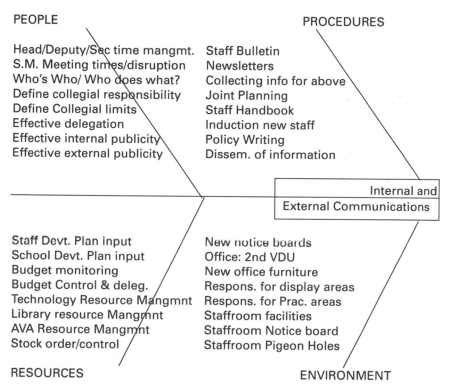

Figure 6.1 The Ishikawa Fishbone

Analysis

The following 'problem areas' were identified from the fishbone and from these, a number of priorities for action identified and agreed by the staff:

People:
Head/deputy/secretary planning time together.

Disruption of senior management meetings.
Staff job descriptions need review.

Procedures:
Staff bulletin arrangements sometimes fail.
Data collection system needed for staff bulletin/newsletters.
Distribution system to parents, staff *and others* needs review.

Resources:
More delegation of budget responsibility and monitoring.
Stock control and ordering system to be tightened.

Environment:
New notice boards needed for main entrance, children's
   entrances and school gate.
Second office VDU needed.
Staffroom needs refurbishing – catering, notice boards and
   furniture.

The questionnaire shown in Figure 6.2 was distributed to all teaching
and ancillary staff and to governors.

Result of Staff Audit:

The statements which provoked the least satisfactory responses were
prioritized, as follows:

a. No parents' notice boards
b. Press and community information
c. Office routines known to staff
d. Where to find documents

e. Staffroom facilities
f. Staff notice board
g. Induction of new staff
h. Who's who? Who does
   what?

Of these, the last three did not merit serious concern but they are
included as being slightly less than an average of 'satisfactory' by
response. It was plain to see that the most significant area where
improvements could be made to good and immediate effect was in
communications, both internally and externally, to parents, governors and the wider community. Following the identification of these
areas, it was agreed that an action plan would be drawn up and that
any items that could not be actioned within six months would be
incorporated into school development planning in the longer term.

Please indicate Excellent (5) Good (4) Adequate (3) Poor (2) Very Poor (1)

No.	Statement	5	4	3	2	1
1	Staff Handbook useful, relevant, up to date.					
2	Staff Notice Board adequate, updated.					
3	Staff information bulletins sufficient, frequent					
4	Staff Pigeon Holes / staffroom furniture					
5	School Brochure attractive, updated					
6	Parents Newsletters frequent, appropriate					
7	Parents' / Visitors notice board					
8	Who's who, who's where, who does what?					
9	Staff- accessible to parents at approp. times.					
10	Head – accessible to parents, visitors.					
11	Head – accessible to staff, Governors.					
12	Office: relevant routines known to parents					
13	Office: relevant routines known to staff					
14	Staff know where to find documents, records, files.					
15	Information / mail for Governors gets there.					
16	Distribution of Mail to staff					
17	Press / community – information / publicity.					
18	Induction of new staff systematic, thorough.					
19	Induction of new children / parents (mid term)					
20	Support / ancillary staff included in above					

Figure 6.2 Staff audit

The Parent Questionnaire

The object of the parent questionnaire was to test out the way that we were perceived by our parents and, in particular, to invite comment or identification in the areas of our weakness. The pastoral and welfare committee, being newly constituted, was anxious to make an impact and responded enthusiastically to the idea of drawing up the questionnaire on the attitudes of parents towards the school.

Figure 6.3 is a copy of the questionnaire sent out to parents, with the results of the questionnaire added, in columns A, B and C, as a percentage of the total replies (113).

PARENTS' QUESTIONNAIRE: ARE YOU PLEASED WITH US?

Please tick one column – column A if you agree, B if you neither agree nor disagree and column C if you disagree:

A) I strongly agree with the statement.
B) I neither agree, nor disagree with the statement.
C) I strongly disagree with the statement.

	STATEMENT	A	B	C
1	My child enjoys coming to school.	80	10	3
2	I am pleased with their progress.	61	24	15
3	I am kept informed how they are getting on.	37	52	11
4	I like the way that things are taught.	49	45	6
5	Parents' meetings help explain about lessons.	42	49	6
6	There are good displays of children's work.	69	28	3
7	School Trips are good value for money.	69	28	3
8	Teachers are always willing to meet me.	76	24	0
9	I always feel welcome in the school.	75	24	1
10	Bad behaviour in school is quickly dealt with.	50	38	12
11	The Order Mark system works well and is fair.	46	36	12
12	My child feels safe in school.	60	35	5
13	The Newsletter keeps me well informed.	89	10	1
14	It's easy to get information when needed.	56	40	4
15	Problems are always dealt with quickly.	53	36	11
16	The uniform is sensible and good value.	87	19	3
17	The Junior and Infant schools work well together.	53	38	9
18	I enjoy the events organised by the PTA.	45	50	5
19	There is enough opportunity to meet with Governors.	25	65	10
20	I hate filling in questionnaires!			

Figure 6.3 Parent questionnaire

The parent questionnaire was sent out with a letter of explanation and children were bribed with a merit mark for returning it! Anonymity was guaranteed to encourage all parents to participate without anxiety. A promise was made to give a prompt response outlining the findings and stating what actual changes would be made in response to the results. It was important that this was seen to be a means to an end and not just a paper exercise.

Results of Parent Questionnaire

One hundred and thirteen replies were received from 180 question-naires sent out. As the number sent out included families with more than one child, these figures represent a 90 per cent return of all *families* at the school. At the end of the week a quick analysis was made of the most immediate findings. The raw results were converted to percentages for easy comparison and the following observations made:

1. Although the overall response showed an overwhelming support for the work of the school we were most urgently concerned with any areas of dissatisfaction that were identifiable. We undertook to highlight and analyse in depth *any* question receiving more than 5 per cent responses that showed dissatisfaction and less than 50 per cent responses indicating satisfaction.
2. We would take account, and investigate in greater detail, any questions where there appeared to be a contradiction of evidence; where more than 50 per cent were well satisfied *but there was also a negative indication greater than 10 per cent.*

An immediate finding under category (2) above concerned the school's order mark system. (An order mark is a slip reporting that a pupil has received a reprimand and is effectively the 'opposite' of a merit mark.) After discussion and consultation with some parents who had chosen to identify themselves, it was felt that the problem was due to misunderstanding the system. It was agreed that in the next newsletter a careful explanation of the policy would be included. Following this a more detailed analysis was published in a four-page document to parents outlining the results, together with comments and an action plan of proposed changes that would be brought about following the survey.

The good behaviour policy was reviewed and 'tidied up' straight away although there were no fundamental changes to it. The order mark system was carefully monitored over a two-week period and found to be both effective and unobtrusive. A majority of children (over 90 per cent) in a straw poll thought it to be fair. Parents were given this information in a subsequent bulletin and copies of the revised good behaviour policy made available.

The remaining items in the action plan were referred on to the senior management team to be included together with the recommendations following from the staff audit into the school development plan with a view to advancing their implementation at the earliest possible convenience. Finally, it was resolved to defer a review of the questionnaire until the Spring term by which time a new year's intake would have settled into the school. A second, smaller questionnaire will then be issued to parents and additionally a more detailed response will be invited from parents and governors by way of an invitation for discussion.

Action Plan

The action plan was drawn up by the senior management team as a result of the parent questionnaire and the staff and governor audit; this is shown in Figure 6.4.

Short-term Objectives (Target Date end of 1993)	Long-term Objectives (Target Date End of 1994)

Curriculum Objectives: (Referenced 'C...')

C1) Completion of Curriculum Mapping (Note a)	C5) All outstanding Policy Documents to be completed.
C2) Documentation for Planning and Recording.(**)	C6) Development of IT Policy and Resourcing. (Note b)
C3) Monitoring delivery of Curriculum (see below)	C7) Development of Resource based Learning to support the Curriculum Map. (Note c)
C4) Review of Good Behaviour Policy (**)	

Ethos – Parent and Community Relationships: (Referenced 'R...')

R1) Notice Boards to be Installed (**)	R4) More Community Involvement (note d)
R2) Brochure to be rewritten (**)	
R3) Improved strategy for Parent Interview evenings and written record. (**)	

Environment Objectives (Referenced 'E...')

E1) Refurbish Staffroom (note e)	E5) Outstanding buildings repairs and Improvements. (Note f)
E2) Litter problem (**)	E6) Replacement of Furniture (Note f)
E3) Staff Chairs / Desks / Filing Cabinets (**)	E7) Development of Practical and Resource areas.
E4) Visitor Reception Area (**)	

Administrative Objectives (Referenced 'A...')

A1) Update and extend Staff
handbook. (**)
A2) Information Collection and
dissemination. for both Staff
and Parents / Governors(**)
A3) Stock Control (**)
A4) New SIMS Terminal (**)
A6) Regular fortnightly SM Meeting (**)

A7) Staff Management
Training

**Follow Up Audit: it is envisaged that a second Audit will be carried out to
review progress and to identify a second phase of priorities.**

Curriculum Priority C3 It is envisaged that the area of Curriculum Quality
will be most specifically targeted for attention in the next audit questionnaire and follow up.

Notes: **   Indicates that the work had been completed (within 6 months of
                the audit).
       a   Completed for 90 per cent of curriculum.
       b and c Coordinators appointed to develop these in 1994.
       d   Pastoral and welfare committee has taken responsibility.
       e   Grant obtained for Spring term completion.
       f   LEA grant applied for.

Figure 6.4 Action plan in response to quality audits

Conclusions

This work was initiated towards the end of the Spring term in 1993
and the results of the parent survey published at the beginning of the
Summer term. Most of the short-term objectives had been met by the
end of the Summer term and by the end of the year, i.e. within six
months of the survey. The remaining short- and long-term objectives
had been incorporated into the school management plan and strategies implemented for their completion. It was agreed that the overall
long-term strategy would focus on more specific issues of
curriculum quality. A major programme of curriculum review had
been in progress at the time these issues of TQM and parental
response were raised and for this reason the questions relating to
curriculum issues were more general.

It would seem to be reasonable, now that the programme of review
is complete, to turn the investigative focus of TQM towards these
issues and evaluate the effectiveness of implementing curriculum
review. The success of this exercise can be judged from a number of

factors: in the first instance, in the complete and open involvement of everyone concerned with an improvement of service – staff, parents, governors *and children*. A number of parents expressed appreciation that the survey had been conducted and that their opinions were clearly valued; secondly, by the analytical nature of the survey in being able to pinpoint and prioritize specific and achievable goals, a clearly defined action plan has been effected. This has given the benefit of some immediate results as well as long-term strategies.

There has been a further benefit, which is less easily quantifiable but nevertheless worthy of mention, and that is the raising of awareness concerning quality and that teamwork and attitude play an important part, in addition to the setting and achieving of goals. Finally, this exercise has not been seen as complete in itself but as the first of an ongoing series of reviews in which different aspects of the management of the school will be the focus, each in their turn. TQM is a continuous process of review and improvement. There is much that is worthy of adopting in our schools, although I suspect that like ourselves, most schools would be selective in their embrace in order to be realistic. Its greatest value is that it offers systems which can give structure in the pursuit of excellence and encouragement by its achievement.

Chapter 7

BS 5750 and Beyond in a Secondary School: A Change for the Best

Mary Healy

Introduction

Over the past five years the management team of our school has had to consciously manage an enormous amount of change and develop strategies which would enable us not only to implement change but also enable the change to become institutionalized. One strategy we have introduced and implemented was the gaining of BS 5750 certification. The aim was not for short-term results but rather an ongoing evolutionary process which would enable a culture of change and development to be established and accepted as the natural way of working.

School Context

The school is situated in Waltham Abbey, West Essex. The town has a population of approximately 18,000 people; it grew from a small market town of 7,000 people in the 1970s as a result of three large housing developments initiated by the then Greater London Council. It is the only secondary school in the town, and has five feeder schools. Due to the falling birth rate the roll of the school has declined over the past ten years from 1,000 to 750 pupils. It is expected to rise again from 1996 onwards.

The present headteacher was appointed in 1982 at a pretty low ebb in the school's fortunes. At the onset his role was authoritative/manipulative. There were lots of 'good' people at the school but they were working in isolation and at times against each other without realizing it. At this stage the headteacher was seen as the fount of all knowledge, setting the agendas, directing the work of task groups, managing the outcomes, strong on exhortation and sending out directives.

During the first five years the notion of teamwork and team responsibility was established. Working parties were set up to initiate a school curriculum review. This enabled us to tie all staff into working in a particular direction. In 1988/9 a major philosophy review was undertaken, this time with open debate whereby a curriculum development plan was created. In 1990/91 this was followed-up with a school effectiveness review which brought together for the first time governors, parents, pupils, community representatives and staff in an exercise which defined for us our development plan.

We had grown up – it was clear that we had developed a school ethos that was open and confident. This was reflected in the changing role of the headteacher which was now one of enabler; a more open management style was evolving. Staff were also now working effectively in formal and informal teams.

Why Did we Seek a Quality Approach?

We didn't know it was called that until later! At the outset the work of Fullan (1991) greatly influenced our thinking. His 'Key themes in improvement' (Figure 7.1) provided us with a focus on which to build our development ideas. Fullan suggests that the management

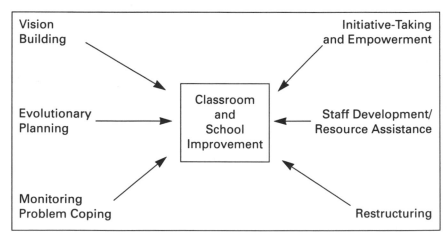

Figure 7.1 Fullan's key themes for improvement

and promotion of change is dependent on six factors. The starting point is *vision building:* it is essential to have a shared and agreed vision and purpose which in turn will facilitate planning. *Planning* should not be viewed as a one-off activity but rather, evolutionary: change takes place over time and must be able to respond to identified needs which will change according to pressures placed upon an institution. Institutions must be prepared and willing to take up new initiatives. Change initially involves an element of uncertainty and anxiety but successful implementation increases the level of *empowerment* of those involved. Because of the element of risk involved it is essential to incorporate ongoing *staff development and resource assistance*. Organizational conditions within and in relation to the school will determine the level of change achieved. Ongoing monitoring, which involves pressure and support, is necessary to recognize and publicize achievements and assist in *problem solving* when necessary and appropriate. Change is a process; it will necessitate individuals altering their ways of thinking and doing. As a consequence change will usually require an element of *restructuring/reorganizing* and this must be recognized and implemented.

We were very conscious of the need to be seen to be succeeding when introducing and implementing a major piece of development work. 'Success breeds success' and we again turned to Fullan for guidance. His 'seven propositions for success' were useful indicators of issues we would have to confront:

- change is learning – loaded with uncertainty
- change is a journey, not a blueprint
- problems are our friends
- change is resource hungry
- change requires the power to manage it
- change is systematic
- all large-scale change is implemented locally

(Fullan and Miles, 1992).

A long debate on what we were trying to do helped us to identify that we were seeking quality in all things, for example,

the way the schools works
what and how we teach
what happens in the classroom
relationships with community, parents, and individuals who have contact with the school.

We wanted ways of assuring quality performance. At this stage in our research we found the work of Deming (1982) provided an insight and useful guide to the concept of quality and the establishment of an environment in which it can flourish. In order to help people understand and put his ideas into practice, Deming produced a list of 14 points for management to consider. However, the idea is not to simply 'adopt' the 14 points shown below, but to create an environment which is fully consistent with and conducive to them, developing a culture that is ongoing, never-ending:

1. constancy of purpose for continual improvement
2. adopt the new philosophy
3. cease dependence on inspection
4. end lowest tender contracts
5. improve every process
6. institute training on the job
7. encourage leadership
8. drive out fear
9. break down barriers
10. eliminate exhortation
11. eliminate arbitrary numerical targets
12. permit pride in workmanship
13. encourage education and self-improvement for everyone
14. top management commitment
(Deming, 1982)

The Quality Improvement Project

In 1989 the school underwent a major philosophy review. One of the main outcomes was to develop further the work of teams within the school, engendering as a central theme a team approach to all aspects of our work. Teacher appraisal has also been identified as one of the key development areas for 1991–2. Once the Department for Education guidelines for teacher appraisal were available it became apparent that the emphasis on line management did not sit comfortably with the team philosophy we were developing.

It was for this reason that we were interested in alternative models for teacher appraisal, built upon a team approach. We wanted to generate our own reporting mechanisms for quality assurance, designed to be consonant with the proposals that were emerging at the time for the new OFSTED inspection framework. We wanted to develop a process of team review which looked to improve quality provision and outcomes in the classroom.

In April 1991 we were invited to be part of the University of Cambridge Institute of Education Research and Development

Project, 'Improving the Quality of Education for All'. The overall aim is to produce and evaluate a model of school development and a programme of support that strengthens a school's ability to provide quality schooling for all its students. The project afforded us a useful vehicle for getting to grips with important school priorities. Involvement also meant that, in working closely with the Institute, we could call on their consultancy expertise. The offer of a fresh set of eyes to look at our work and performance could not be overlooked.

The school thus had an internal drive towards a particular type of quality assurance management system and had external support and impetus. The internal drive is essential; the external support of great value.

Getting Started

Staff agreed in principle to the project which would attempt to develop strategies and ways of working that would have an impact on the quality of education we offered our pupils. A task group was formed to steer the project, with membership on a voluntary basis. Fourteen staff came forward who covered the spectrum of roles and responsibilities within the school. The group visited selected businesses throughout the country which were noted for their track record in quality. Nine organizations were visited and, using an agreed format, the group collated their findings and placed them in a context appropriate for the school. Three quality improvement models were proposed. Members of the task group made a formal presentation to staff and one model was selected.

At the same time that the quality improvement process was developed, the whole-school community (staff – teaching, support, ancillary – governors and parents) came together to reaffirm the school philosophy and write our mission statement and a series of vision statements. These underwent a series of fine-tuning until we ended up with nine that all parties were happy with. They are critical within the quality improvement process as they form the backcloth, the frame within which teams root their work.

King Harold Grant Maintained School

Our Mission is to be :-

Committed to Excellence

Pioneers and Leaders in Education

Our Vision is:

- To have a clear view of where we are going
- To strive constantly to recognise the achievements of all pupils
- To be committed to academic excellence, encouraging staff and pupils to achieve their highest potential
- To provide a happy working atmosphere for all and to develop a high sense of self esteem and self respect
- To employ excellent staff who are highly motivated and committed
- To have an innovative approach to the curriculum
- To be committed to education as a life-long process
- To develop partnerships with parents, local business and the wider community

(KHGMS, 1993).

The Quality Improvement Process

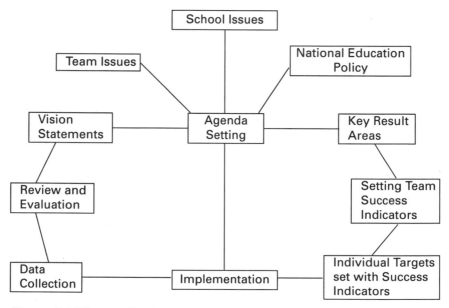

Figure 7.2 The quality improvement process

The quality improvement process requires a team to develop a vision statement and to identify one or two major targets that align with the vision statement. These targets become the focus for the team over the next few weeks/months, a time-scale having been agreed by the team. In relation to the target areas selected, the team have to come to a shared understanding as to what good quality practice would look like; agreement through negotiation would be sought so that all staff know what it is as a team they are striving for – performance indicators together with evidence that would be needed. Within the team, target staff would then set clear individual targets, again with performance indicators they would need to meet in order to demonstrate that their individual contributions had led to quality improvement and the achievement of the team's targets. These would be formally logged, strategies explored that would enable the team to realize its goals and a formal review meeting set when all team members bring appropriate evidence. The evidence substantiates that the targets, both individual and collective, have been achieved. The outcomes from the team review meeting are formally recorded which a) recognize how far the team have got, and b) help generate the agenda for the next stage of development.

The interest and strength generated by this model lies in the fact that throughout the process control lies with the team: the process itself unleashes the potential that all staff have to apply their experience to solve problems facing their team. The process aims wherever possible to encourage staff to make professional decisions and to generate solutions to identified problems that face them. Autonomy to do this is developed within the team.

BS 5750

On our visits to business and industry it became apparent that one way of ensuring delivery of quality was to accredit the systems in a business to BS 5750 standard. As a school we realized the tremendous potential that existed in BS 5750 and TQM. We believed TQM could be adapted to a school context; it is a high ideal, but we felt it had tremendous implications for the culture of the institution: a) in how things were done; b) in how it enmeshed approach, attitude, aspiration and how people felt about the institution within which they work.

We worked to increase the effectiveness of teams and to generate self-managing teams which have an understanding of their collective and individual responsibility for delivering quality in their area.

Quality improvement in the way that teams operate would be ineffective unless we firmed up the school context in which it would operate. It would be like building a structure on sand unless we had a common understanding of how we as a school functioned. BS 5750 provided the structure. As part of the standard requirements we had to determine what we perceived our product to be. We decided that it would be the delivered curriculum. We felt this would be beneficial in that: a) it would alleviate the frustration and irritation that staff may have felt in the past when 'things' have not worked properly, or had broken down; b) it would attempt to make sure that everyone knew what was meant to happen and what an individual's specific responsibilities were in ensuring that the systems work effectively to ensure a quality delivery of the curriculum.

An analysis was made identifying the key systems and processes that operate within the institution and are critical if the institution is to be effective. This involved tying processes down and defining, in BS 5750 terms, the scope, purpose, responsibility, procedure, records and proformas of the systems and how they are to be monitored and evaluated. It would be one of the keys to improving quality as all staff would know:

- exactly how a system operates;
- what happens and how;
- who is involved and responsible;
- how the system is monitored and evaluated.

INSET days were used to begin the process of writing the systems. Procedures were developed for people who had a direct responsibility for servicing these systems to be able to verify them. Some 70 systems have been established that have a bearing on the quality of the delivered curriculum. This was an extremely useful exercise as staff became very aware of what their individual and collective responsibility was in making these systems work effectively.

All systems have to be audited to see how well they are working and to ensure that where they are not, strategies are planned to rectify the shortfalls. A rolling programme of training will ensure that all staff will be trained as internal auditors and will have carried out this function. This is to avoid the notion that an audit is done *to* staff by a discrete group of colleagues, but rather that we all have a collective responsibility to ensure the effective running of systems and as such, we are all responsible for ensuring that this happens.

Impact of our work on quality

Building shared values leads to a greater awareness and understanding of what makes for *quality.*

We are constantly reinforcing the *culture* whereby self-managing teams understand increasingly their individual and collective responsibility for delivering quality in their area.

We now have *mechanisms* to report on our quality assurance process. This is particularly pertinent in light of the new inspection framework.

The school has become more *effective* with greater collective accountability and awareness of responsibilities. It has enabled us to *manage:*

- development planning;
- making explicit what we are about as an institution;
- marketing the school more effectively;
- the opening up of people's practice in a supportive environment;
- the sharing of ideas and successful approaches.

Promoting the idea of *leadership* throughout the school. (Formal team leaders, task and steering team leaders, internal auditors).

Devolving greater *autonomy* to teams, enpowering and enabling them to set their own priorities for improvement and development.

All *teams* have a quality improvement process that can be applied to any aspect of their work.

Teams are working within an agreed broad *framework* provided by the mission and vision statements.

All staff have a clear understanding of their individual and *collective responsibility* for delivering quality.

What have we achieved?

The quality improvement process is in place and is becoming embedded in the working life of the school; we are moving from the developmental phase to the institutionalization of the process.

BS 5750 certification gives our parents and community confidence in what we are about and in what we stand for. The standard ratifies and acknowledges quality –

in the way the school is run,
in the way the educational processes are organized,

in the way we are constantly seeking incremental improvement in all aspects of our work.

It has enabled us to ensure quality reporting mechanisms that demonstrate quality delivery in the classroom.

What do we do Now?

Quality is dynamic, it never stays the same. We have identified five issues which will form the focus of our next development phase:

- *reinforce autonomy in team working:*
  to achieve quality you must empower people to take responsibility. By developing staff skills to solve problems in their teams the school management team can concentrate on strategic planning and leading the development thrust, i.e. achieving the goals of the institution;
- *remove the hierarchical structure through the introduction of a flatter management structure:*
  the introduction of a two layer management structure which operates within three 'house' teams across the school;
- *reorganize the school structure to reflect quality developments*:
  introducing three formal 'house' teams which bring pastorals and curriculum responsibilities together; using project based task/steering groups to facilitate ongoing development work;
- *the introduction of quality mangers:*
  to facilitate the application and improvement of the quality improvement process;
- *delegating more of the financial budget to teams:*
  the autonomy will only be achieved when teams have the resources to implement and manage the process of change themselves.

Lessons learned

Our quality journey began many years ago and will continue for many more. We have only reached the end of the beginning. For any institution considering the quality path a number of issues must be addressed:

full staff understanding is essential;
financial outlay has to be considered;
the process must be a whole-school priority with resources of time, staff and cash devoted to it;

'all staff' means teaching, support and ancillary personnel;
time-bound task groups with specific tasks and functions are
required;
commitment to quality improvement must be constant and come
from senior management; words are cheap – it is behaviour that
counts;
it must be emphasized that it is a programme of development for a
decade.

Total quality goes beyond the team. The challenge is how we break
through barriers and succeed in institutionalization. That involves
embedding a culture within, rather than imposing a structure upon,
our schools.

Chapter 8
Getting a Secondary School Ready for OFSTED Inspection

Paul Barras

Introduction

A quality improvement team was established to examine the implications of OFSTED inspection for the school's assessment, reporting and recording (ARR) policy and practices. The goal was to make improvements in that area which would raise quality in advance of inspection. The group looked to develop procedures which are accurate and consistent and which are easily and diplomatically applied within the school.

Context

St John Fisher School is a successful and oversubscribed Catholic, mixed comprehensive school. There are 1,200 pupils between the ages of 11 and 18. It gained Grant Maintained Status on 1 April 1993, a move prompted by the potential opportunity this afforded to extend the limited accommodation on two separate sites. I have been deputy head in the school for five years with responsibilities which include an oversight of assessment practices within the school.

Focus

A number of factors influenced the decision, taken at senior management level, to review the school ARR policy and practice. Our main concern was to ensure that the existing policy, introduced two terms previously, was being implemented effectively and appropriately so as to ensure high quality teaching and learning. At that time, in common with most schools, we were familiarizing ourselves with the OFSTED *Handbook for the Inspection of Schools* (1993) and agreed that the best way to prepare for our inspection, whenever it should come, was by systematically 'doing it to ourselves' before the inspectors arrived at the door. In line with this thinking, various quality assurance mechanisms designed to ensure good practice were in place. We had no reason for panic measures: on the contrary, we focused on assessment and its related issues because it was an area already identified for development in the plans for the forthcoming year. In particular, it had been agreed to extend to Years 7, 8 and 9 the procedures established further up the school for pupil self-assessment, for profiling and reporting attainment. An audit of teacher and pupil opinion during the accreditation process to award the Record of Achievement had shown that procedures whereby, for example, pupils evaluate their learning and set agreed targets with their teachers, were working well in Years 10 and 11. Nevertheless, it was expedient to judge whether these procedures, as described in the school's ARR policy, were in need of refinement before extending them to the rest of the school. We needed to gauge the extent to which our staff felt capable of operating the current policy and to examine whether current policy allowed us to meet the demands of external regulation and the requirements of the National Curriculum.

The aims of the review were thus to develop and to refine the ARR policy and, where necessary, to make it clearer and its procedures more manageable and sustainable for our staff. In order to begin this process, evidence would be needed of teachers' knowledge and understanding of the assessment policy and the extent to which their assessment practice complied with the current policy. Of course, evidence of the kind OFSTED inspectors would eventually be looking for would be gathered. One can argue that the possession of such information before inspection is a very effective means of preparation: the school is thus better able to determine its own priorities for action and staff retain control of their own agenda. Inspection in these circumstances is not to be seen as a threat, but rather an opportunity (Ormston and Shaw, 1993) for schools to gain an insight into whether their procedures are operating as planned. OFSTED inspection, we are advised (*TES*, 25 June 1993), should be used as a tool for improvement and be viewed as part of an on-going process, linked to the school's development planning cycle.

The Quality Improvement Team

Total Quality Management, with its principle of driving out fear and its commitment to building 'participative management' (Robson,

1988, p.42) provides an attractive counterweight to the pressure placed on teachers and schools by outside inspection. In Deming's view (1988), by involving staff in the task of continuous improvement without blaming them for any shortcomings, there is a greater chance of assuring quality than by seeking to eliminate problems through inspection. We would all agree on the need to build in our schools a positive climate for change and to encourage the belief amongst staff that they possess the competence and skills to meet the needs of pupils, their parents and society at large. Deming is surely correct in arguing that inspection is a costly way to raise quality: it does not attack the problem at source but only looks at outcomes and tends to harm staff morale (Walton, 1991). TQM offers an alternative notion of building quality by the creation of an improvement team with the purpose of reviewing practice, and by making use of, for example, rigorous and positive methods for the collection and analysis of data.

In this case, an improvement team was already to hand and well suited to its task: the school assessment committee. It is a consultative standing committee of 12 which has grown out of the Record of Achievement validation group. Staff members represent areas of the curriculum, they make recommendations to heads of department, and they have become increasingly confident with the complexities of the assessment scene across the school as a whole. As its chairperson, I saw the review as an opportunity for me to develop the team by giving its members the task of appraising the workings of a key policy in their own areas of curriculum expertise. In this way, they would gain further insight into the difficulties which colleagues in other areas were facing. It would also benefit the team as a whole to work together to make mutually agreed changes to procedures and to find areas of success to celebrate, as we had previously worked hard to develop an agreed approach amongst staff as a whole. Moreover, the review process would confer a sense of empowerment to team members; their involvement in defining targets for future development would enable them to feel more confident as 'progress chasers' and the team would be better able to play the role of 'quality assurance' monitors for their own departmental teams.

When I first explained the format of the review and the steps we would be taking at our May meeting, it was not surprising that I found no real enthusiasm for the task! There was agreement, however, that a review was necessary, it was timely and the results would be interesting. The general feeling was that it would be useful to know what difficulties staff were encountering with the current policy. Two further meetings were arranged before the end of term and we made it our target to have a revised policy in place for September. Only later, when the review process came to be evaluated, was it discovered that members of the team already had concerns. In at least one department there was worry being generated about the prospect of a review because of their problems in putting the current policy into practice and the fear that this would be revealed by the proposed teacher audit, with its members being shown in a bad light. They decided that they would have to face this issue before the audit and a special meeting of that department was hurriedly convened. The process had immediately given rise to some understandable fears and possible distrust. With hindsight, some of these concerns may have been allayed at this preliminary stage by assuring the team more forcibly that the results of the audit would not be used to identify specific teachers or departments which may not be conforming in their practice to the assessment policy.

The Quality Audit

The team members were given some 'homework' to do before our next meeting: I was relying on them to distribute a questionnaire to staff in their curriculum areas, to explain its purpose, and to chase its return before our next meeting. The questionnaire was not ready at that time, however. Later, a memo was attached to remind team members of the purpose of the review and to explain the audit. Some misunderstandings could have been avoided and some concerns allayed if, when the questionnaires were eventually distributed, there had been included a copy of these notes for every member of staff. An intervening staff development day gave ample opportunity for staff to complete the audit, following discussion in their departmental groups. The questionnaire (see Figure 8.1) contained 20 statements; scoring was done on a 5–1 scale depending on the extent to which one agreed with each statement. Teachers added up their scores and checked what their total meant in terms of their conformance with the assessment policy. Many appreciated this approach and were interested to find out how they were doing; a few staff were critical of this method because they thought it encouraged some to 'cheat' in order to get a good score! It had not occurred to me that there would be such a 'competitive edge'. Others said that since all the statements did not apply to their curriculum area, they were unable to score as highly as some of their colleagues.

The memo and the questionnaire reflected the TQM approach;

TEACHER AUDIT

PURPOSE OF QUESTIONNAIRE: to establish the extent to which present policy is established.

GUIDANCE: Complete the following by drawing a circle round the number which indicates your degree of agreement or disagreement with each statement.

*(NC)–National Curriclum	Strongly Agree	Agree	Unsure	Disagree	Strongly Disagree
My current practice enables me to make an accurate assessment of each pupil	5	4	3	2	1
Each pupil gets a clear explanation of what is to be assessed	5	4	3	2	1
My assessment activities motivate pupils and facilitate their achievement	5	4	3	2	1
All pupils get quick feedback on the quality of their work	5	4	3	2	1
*(NC)–Assessment criteria are presently linked to the programmes of study and the statements of attainment	5	4	3	2	1
The assessment criteria are applied consistently in my marking	5	4	3	2	1
My assessments are used to inform my planning for the class	5	4	3	2	1
My assessments are used to inform my planning for individual pupils	5	4	3	2	1
I use assessment to give feedback to pupils and I use my comments to set new targets for individuals	5	4	3	2	1
There is an agreed approach to marking pupils' work in my department	5	4	3	2	1
The marks which I give are determined by the extent to which the pupil has shown s/he knows, understands and can do what has been asked of her/him	5	4	3	2	1
The Department's record-keeping system is manageable and I am up-to-date with my records	5	4	3	2	1
Pupils have regular and structured opportunities to record their own strengths and weaknesses and to set targets for themselves	5	4	3	2	1
*(NC)–My records are supported by the retention of evidence for the purpose of end of Key Stage reports	5	4	3	2	1
My records are passed on to the pupil's next teacher	5	4	3	2	1
I make use of records passed on to me	5	4	3	2	1
We make use of methods to ensure consistent assessment standards in my Department. For example, we compare and agree our marking. There is moderation in NC as well as GCSE	5	4	3	2	1

Current assessment practice is known and understood by all my pupils	5	4	3	2	1
The pupils have access to and understand our records	5	4	3	2	1
Our current practice is known and followed by all the members in the department	5	4	3	2	1

You may add up your total and enter it here..........................

85 and above: you have established the present policy: well done!
70–84: Quite good, but you must look at the ARR policy and plan to adapt your procedures this term to meet school and NC requirements
60–69: caution; suggests that there is much work to be done and you must be in contact immediately with me
59 and below: ouch! you are out of touch with the current approach to reviewing and monitoring pupils' progress

Figure 8.1 Reviewing and monitoring the progress of individual pupils

many staff appreciated being consulted about the workings of a school policy in this way and the opportunity it provided to air their views. One department made a very strong response complaining that the requirement not to mark pupils' work on overall impression was unworkable: in this case, the questionnaire had led to a discussion about the broader aspects of the policy, not only those areas specifically identified by the audit. Another department drew a more fundamental conclusion from the exercise, namely that their procedures were too cumbersome and did not always serve the purpose for which they were designed.

From the results there was reason to celebrate how far in general the policy was understood and being followed. But, as some had predicted, the audit revealed a good deal of inconsistent practice across and between curriculum areas. The team gained much from the exercise. For example, it had revealed that in one department there was a clear dichotomy between teachers in their practice and it identified specific areas which needed to be urgently addressed. The questionnaire had proved to be successful and I would make a case for the technique to be used again to examine other policies and procedures.

'Fishboning'

The results of the questionnaire helped us to pinpoint the areas in the ARR policy most in need of change or clarification. A tally chart was drawn up showing the overall scores relating to each statement, to help the team to draw their own conclusions. Nevertheless, it was

important that we did not get bogged down in detailed recrimina-
tions. In the spirit of TQM, we had to move forward and, by positive
means, explore the root causes for non-conformance and set corrective action in the form of a revised policy that was more helpful to
staff. Conscious, too, of the importance TQM attaches to the role of
the leader, I was insistent that we would not waste time and under-
mine morale by being too self-critical. So it was quickly agreed that
essentially we could express the problem as 'the inconsistent application of policy'. In true TQM fashion, a fishbone, cause-effect, or
Ishikawa diagram (West-Burnham, 1992, p.57), was drawn on the
board, providing a structure to record a brainstorming session. It was
planned to use this technique to help us identify the causes of the
problem, to seek to relate these causes to one another and to decide
on which of these common factors had most effect. Later evaluation
revealed that at least one member of the team was mystified by this
particular approach. For him, the diagram was confusing and was no
more help in defining the causes of the problem than a normal brainstorming activity would have been. He said that it had wasted time
and it was an unnecessary strain on the chairperson. (Needless to
say, I had been careful not to use the term 'Ishikawa' at any stage!)

My opening remarks at this meeting were prepared along TQM
lines: 'the failure of a process says more about the system and its
designer than the people who operated it' (West-Burnham, 1992,
p.47). The argument was advanced that procedures have to be developed and improved by the teams that will have to implement them
and they must be written in response to the needs of pupils, teachers
and the National Curriculum. The phrase 'meeting our customers'
needs' was not used, but quality was spoken of in terms of the
importance of doing things right and of creating a situation in which
we could all conform. The audit showed that, both as departments
and as individuals, there was a worrying level of non-conformance in
some key areas. In an attempt to 'drive out fear', it was argued that
this was the result of the procedures not being understood, being
inappropriate or being badly designed and not because of people
failing to do the job properly. As TQM would have us do, I was
seeking to remove the person from the problem.

Although there was some disagreement amongst the team as to
what the audit really revealed, with some criticism of the ambiguity
of some of the statements which were likely to have given
misleading scores, the response to my remarks was very positive. It
was I as the chairperson who had little to fear; one could conclude
that, in the haste to define and to win recognition of a problem to

rectify, a valuable opportunity was lost at this stage to celebrate the team's success. In fact, this would have acted as a further spur to make the team more determined to seek the reasons for non-conformance across the staff as a whole. Discussion then focused on the pressure of time for the classroom teacher to implement the current procedures. It was felt that the policy was not specific enough and some of its demands were unrealistic. Two related causes for the problem thus gained consensus: the policy and shortage of time. We did not complete the fishbone diagram; the team members were asked to complete their own versions and to report back at our next specially convened meeting in which we would produce a revised ARR policy.

Setting Corrective Action

When team members finally reported back there was common agreement that the staff had not sufficiently understood the current policy and that its procedures needed to be more helpful. The policy had not fully taken into account the needs of staff. Later evaluation of the process confirmed that there was an appreciation of the notion of 'customer satisfaction' in the sense that the rest of the staff were users of a product developed by the team. With this in mind, we proceeded to look at each part of the policy, seeking to clarify all the procedures which had to be followed to conform to LEA guidelines and government requirements, focusing particularly on those for the reviewing and monitoring of the progress of individual pupils. At each stage we were asking ourselves whether the change we were proposing was operable. The result was a policy much altered in tone and its demands much more clearly defined. This was a very intensive session in which all members took part; it was productive because we had defined our own terms of reference and because of the high level of motivation within the group. It was intensely practical and very tiring for the chairperson! One very important moment arose when it was mentioned that only 15 months earlier we had still been in the process of thinking about a common policy, at which, quite spontaneously, smiles erupted with comments about how much had been achieved in the interim. At the end, feelings of satisfaction and of being in control were expressed – sentiments which have recently not often been in evidence in schools dealing with the area of assessment.

Testing the Results and Completing the Circle

The changes were later accepted by the relevant senior groups within the school and the policy itself was distributed to all staff in September as planned. At the beginning of the review the target for success had been set as having established a revised policy which was agreed and acted on by all staff: 'zero defects'! It was necessary, however, to establish smaller scale success criteria to enable the team to check progress and to celebrate achievement on the way to this goal. Therefore, a pupil audit is planned for later this year, involving members of the team in some structured interviews with a representative sample so as to illuminate the results of the audit. The process we have conducted is also built into our annual assessment development plan where there are agreed smaller steps. The plan is to review the revised policy next year in order then to establish the level of conformance and to judge whether the changed procedures outlined in the new policy have rectified the problems identified this year.

Chapter 9

Acting up – Quality Assurance in A Level Theatre Studies and GCSE Drama

Myrna Harris

Introduction

It was everywhere this year. When the windscreen broke on Christmas Eve, I knew I was dealing with quality assurance as I drank the repair company's coffee and filled in an embarrassingly detailed questionnaire about the poor chap who was sweeping up my broken glass. What could I award him but a row of 'A's? The confident smile on his face assured me that he worked in a 'no blame' culture. When my landlady, who teaches part-time FE students gave me a gilt-edged executive desk diary, a gift from one who works in industry, it had the house rules for quality assurance printed on the flyleaf. In September, we had a day's quality training before the school's quality audit took place in the autumn term. Don't imagine I have had enough of it. It has given me results at school; one day, ideas I borrowed from industrial safety check-lists and calendars may save somebody's life in the school hall.

Reading case studies about quality circles of the kind presented by Robson (1984) gave me the idea that the management of A Level Theatre Studies and GCSE Drama in school could benefit from some parallel thinking to that which now frequently occurs in industry. There was a place for the input of quality circles at different levels, and these would benefit the students. At their best, they could raise the standard of life and happiness for all interested parties and they would help the drive towards better examination results.

System Products and Quality Students

The experience of industry shows that quality circles form, grow, have their day and die. Margaret Attwood (1986) reviewed the characteristics of British quality circles as they were shaping up in 1986, and these have not changed greatly. People, individual talents, move on, the driving force of a particular circle goes. This is natural; it is part of the organic growth of a company. When individuals stop meeting for the purpose, it does not mean that quality circles fail. We live in a culture that encourages the movement of individual labour through market forces. We are no longer employed in a job for life. Talented people are expected to move on if they want promotion. Somehow, a quality circle has to fit this culture.

In education, not only do the staff move: students move on in waves. No sooner is a quality circle formed than it has to disband. On most educational courses, no product is made: students study. Locked up in their own mind, they regurgitate what is necessary at the right time; they do it competitively, alongside others. In the process of their making, manufactured goods do not fall in love; their fathers do not die nor their mothers run away; their brothers are not detained at Her Majesty's pleasure, nor do their sisters fall into the hands of evil religious cults. All of those things, and worse, can happen to a student in an academic year. The process by which even self-destructive and bloody-minded students mature into responsible professionals, despite their emotional scars and hang-ups, is still a mystery. They are not products of a system. Even so, there is a place for the Kite Mark and BS 5750 in education.

A Place for the Kite Mark and every Kite Mark in its Place

In industry, a quality circle can only work in a total quality environment, where trained top management comprehend fully the nature and the components of the power with which they are empowering others, and their reasons for doing it. The members of a quality circle have to be trained to think constructively for it to work. It cannot work in an atmosphere of internal competitiveness, cynicism or politics. Douglas McGregor's once-fashionable 'Theory X and Theory Y' of management, which deals with nurture versus the stick, is a useful philosophical guide for all managers. Theory X gives low expectations about people in general, a belief that most people are lazy and uninterested and have to be bribed, threatened and coerced into activity to achieve organizational objectives. Theory Y, 'the Japanese way' requires trust and belief in the best motives of the work force.

To work, quality circles have to choose their own work problem to study. It must not be management's golden opportunity to impose more work on the employees, nor must it be the employees' circle for grumbling about the management. The union-led quality circle that decided to study why there was no pay-rise this year was not a quality circle, for quality circles are not pressure groups. They are places where extraordinarily creative things happen. Firms that are traditionally hostile to the work force have great difficulty in establishing a quality circle. At Alcock Plate, early quality circles were suspended: top management and trade unions were against it; there were redundancies and company restructuring, high labour turnover, lack of cooperation from middle and first-line managers, and failure by circle leaders to find time to organize meetings (Robson, 1988). A company that has a tradition of nurturing employees' talent is more likely to succeed in establishing a quality circle that produces solutions of universal benefit.

Encircling Quality

A growing number of articles in the educational press report individual schools following, particularly, Deming's theories. Training is offered to schools by the Deming Society. In 'The Holy Grail' Brooks (1992) pinpoints the nature of change of culture needed in schools for this to work. It is almost a spiritual experience and quality circles are only one visible, practical part of it. It seems that education, traditionally peopled by the givers in society, is ripe for using quality circles as a matter of course. During the past six months, I have set up two of them in two different schools.

Last year's A Level Theatre Studies students left the school, as I did, and have scattered to the four winds. Almost every one of them sent me a Christmas card this year. I was not surprised, for they see themselves as 'quality' students who know what they are doing, why they are doing it and that we were all participants in something quite special last year.

At the end of their course, after their examinations were over, I called them all together and gave them a questionnaire. The contents of the questionnaire are unimportant. What matters is that, after writing a few facile remarks, they began to respond. Did we really want to know their opinions? Now? After the course was over? Yes: we really did want to know. Looking back, did they really get the course they chose? How could we have made things better and easier, altogether more satisfactory? Did they have any regrets?

The message that came back to us was that, although the course had been described to the students during their fifth year, and more than one had taken it because they could work with girls for a change and it would be a diversion from the grind of more formal subjects, most had no real conception of the diversity of techniques, skills and talents needed to do well in the course. Most wished they had had more previous experience of drama and of theatre. Most now felt that they had only dabbled in a fascinating world that they would never belong to: and that seemed like a regret. Certainly they had become a group by this time, a sub-culture of the school, members of a secret society who knew the strange, dark world of the back stage and the powerful mysteries of the lighting gallery. Thrown onto their own resources more than they had ever imagined, they had, in turn, hated the staff for throwing them into high profile situations, their personalities bared and dressed in (metaphorically) yellow tights; and loved us for pulling them through the ordeal to an adrenalin high.

As a teaching staff, we decided firmly what we had suspected all along:

- that the students ought to be given more information about the course and selected even more carefully than before: in effect, pre-selected for success;
- that the students should have more structured consultation with us: not just in parents' evenings, but at other, informal times;
- that rooms and facilities should be looked at constantly and in structured ways for their efficiency in relation to the course;
- that there was a place for two quality circles, one of students and teachers, the other of teachers of the course and all significant others who were involved with Theatre Studies;
- that the profile of Theatre Studies throughout the school should be raised, because it is a showcase for the school;
- that Drama should be integrated from age 11 in such a way that it was apparent who was suitable for A Level Theatre Studies before the option was taken;
- that suitability for the course would also be on the grounds of integration with life and career plans of the student, and that the students would be counselled by appropriate staff early on with regard to this.

There was nothing revolutionary or time-consuming about these ideas. It was our focus upon them within a school striving for total quality that made the difference.

Out of this came a useful check-list calendar of key events in the school's theatre year, which included dates for quality circle meetings and dates for routine health and safety checks of equipment and premises. It was a calendar which could be used and adapted by any of the teachers of the course, and it was particularly useful to new teaching staff (see Appendix 9.1).

Quality Quality Circles

Quality circle diagrams, continually redrawn, were useful for focusing our attention on the diversity of people who are involved in putting on the school's autumn production and the final practical examinations (see Figure 9.1). In the routine of devising them I realized what diversity of ability, talent and goodwill was available once structured parental contribution was encouraged and employed.

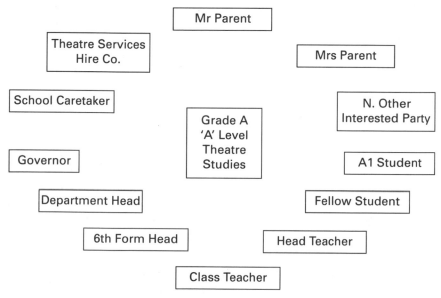

In normal circumstances, all of these people will never meet together around a table – think of the cost – think of the breaking of conventions – but in a quality circle, if all were determined upon a Grade A for A1 Student, they might.
'Had we but world enough and time...' of course, they do not need to meet literally around a table. They only need the will to share a common, focused purpose.

Figure 9.1 Focus of attention and orientation

The quality circle in my present school meets very briefly when the parents collect the girls after Sunday rehearsals. They are encouraged not to get cold waiting in the car, but to sit and watch rehearsals. Normally, parents and students meet to be informed of progress by school teachers. In the quality circle, parents meet to discuss the script, and for the present production, take an active part in its censorship and its emendations. Gone are the days when the caretaker opened the doors with, 'Tell me when you're finished and I'll lock up'. Now he takes an active part. Issues are hammered out between us all before they become major stumbling blocks to success. On the whole, the students feel liberated, more confident, less isolated, less oppressed by the demands made of them. No report will be written as result of the quality circle meeting to

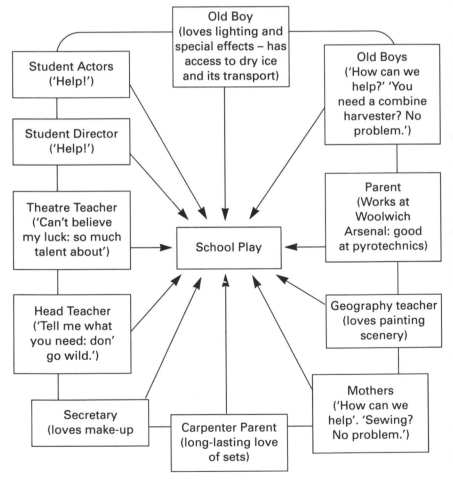

Talent needs direction. They need to meet to integrate design.

Figure 9.2 The school play – quality circle

discuss what is to be done in order to achieve the best production possible this year. Traditional quality circles study a specific problem which the members have isolated and they send their written report to management. The Theatre Studies quality circles have informally and creatively studied immediate problems concerned with the production of a single play (see Figure 9.2). The reports have been verbal and cumulative because few members of the circle are employees of the institution. They have, however, led to measurable qualities of excellence. By Easter, the quality circle has done its job and crept quietly away. Items on the check-list calendar (Appendix 9.1) are ticked off one by one as tasks are carried out. Disasters waiting to happen have been prevented.

Deliberately breaking down the glass wall between teaching staff, parents and support staff is never going to be easy. Formal relationships have to be given up and then rebuilt; and there can be awkwardness in this process. There is no retreating behind formality and mystery once the process has begun. Quality circles without formal training are likely to falter; but what will parents and teachers not do to secure better grades for their young people? Theatre Studies and Drama are subjects where the success of one student is greatly dependent upon that of another. There is a place, even in our overcrowded school curriculum, for techniques of TQM to be taught in school time. If it is to succeed, then certainly our students will welcome it as a familiar friend later on in their business and professional lives. The sooner quality techniques are incorporated into the

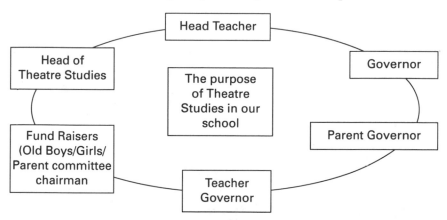

Occasional meeting; making a statement as to the purpose and value of Theatre Studies in the school. This allows budgets to be made without resentment or misunderstanding.

Figure 9.3 Raising the profile of Theatre Studies

work culture of our young people the better.

Yet another sort of quality circle works well to defend or extend òne's little empire. Raising the profile of Theatre Studies is a necessity if funding is to be protected, support is to be assured, appreciation elicited and the best acquired for the students (see Figure 9.3). But enough of this micro-politicing. Either quality management is another in a long series of North Atlantic fads to hit our shores or it is a dynamic and effective device to be used in the raising of standards. Like magic, it will fail to work in an atmosphere of cynicism. Who needs cynicism in education, anyway?

Appendix 9.1

Checklist Calendar – Dates to be filled in each academic year

Summer Term

School management should review the school's profile with regard to Theatre, viz. examinations available, extra-curricular Theatre provision.

The team of teachers who will be teaching the course should meet to devise a timetable for the delivery of the course. The choice of texts should be confirmed and any books required should be ordered. The school librarian should be involved in the provision of peripheral texts which the students may consult. Members of staff should make provision for any personal books to be lent through the librarian.

Prospective students of the course should be invited to a meeting of those teachers who will be teaching the course and the careers adviser. The entry requirements of the course should be explained, a clear picture of the day-to-day requirements should be explained as well as the uses of this 'A' Level in further and higher education and in job prospects.

In a separate meeting of staff, those who are still interested in joining the course should be vetted through their school performance and through an audition if necessary. Their possible choice in the 'special option paper' should be discussed. It should be established at this stage that the pupil would benefit from the 'A' Level and that it fits with his chosen career plans. 'A' Level Theatre Studies must not be chosen by weak students simply because the subject is untried.

In August or early September, once the G.C.S.E. results are known, a meeting of staff, parents and prospective students would discuss what is required. Details of the syllabus would be outlined. It would be pointed out that Theatre Studies involves leaving students alone for periods of time to organise and rehearse. At times, students would need to work on Saturdays and Sundays. Loose, old clothing would need to be brought to classes. During the period of the school play in October, which would contribute to experience needed for 'A' Level Practical work, students may need to spend a disproportionate amount of time on Theatre Studies; at other times of the year, when texts are studied, much less would need to be done. Pupils have a personal responsibility with regard to each others' 'A' Level successes because they work closely together and their performances at all levels are integrated. Students should, at this stage, be allowed to ask that pupils with a reputation for disruption and immaturity be excluded from the course as part of the consultative stage.

Summer Recess

Theatre safety checks must be undertaken by an independent specialist firm. This pays great dividends in matters of insurance and in the prevention of contingencies. Theatre electrics must be healthy or they must be shut down. Major works based on continuously updated reports made during the year would be acted upon according to earlier major management decisions during this time.

Winter Term

Checking of equipment by Theatre staff. Theatre safety lecture should be given to students.

Texts are studied according to the schedule agreed. Frequent team-teacher meetings. Syllabus is checked. Examination board instructions are checked. Queries are cleared up with the examination board.

Mid-term meeting with students and team teachers in an informal setting to discuss the course, to air fears and worries, to focus attention on the term's tasks.

Reports to parents and students should not contain surprises. Assessment should be integrated with teaching. Time should be given for occasional tutorials with individual students, identifying strengths and weaknesses in the subject. Syllabus options should be tailored carefully to the individual students.

The School Play forms an integral part of the learning process which contributes to the 'Practicals' paper in 'A' Level Theatre. It is also a high-profile showcase of the school. This involves co-operation and the spirit of empathy amongst all the staff. Each school play is different and makes different demands upon different individuals. A school play timetable of auditions, rehearsals, provision of resources, printing, budgeting and ticketing needs to be drawn up by the staff and students at the earliest possible moment. The timetable should be displayed in the Drama Room. The teaching staff need to be sensitive to the degrees of responsibility given to the students. Frequent meetings of the team of Theatre teachers need to take place.

Mock examinations should be based on the questions to be found in past public examination papers. It should be explained to students before the mock examinations are taken that the marking will be at the standard of the 'A' Level (or the G.C.S.E.). For the first year students of a two year course, the examination should either be marked to the public examination standard or it should be marked to the 'first-year' expectation standard. Before taking the examination, the students should be aware of which benchmark is being used.

Individual time should be given for 'debriefing' following the mock examination. It is an essential part of the learning process that students should not be left in a mood of discouragement following the examination. Both the classroom teacher and the person who marked the papers should be available for this essential part of the course.

Spring Term

Final texts are taught to the second year students. New texts are taught to the first year students.

Practical 'A' Level examinations are taken at the end of the term. First year students should be encouraged to be an audience when these examiantions take place in order to know how the examinations are co-ordinated and conducted. Some of the first year students may be asked to be actors in the productions of the second years. This provides good practice and raises standards of the first year students.

Rooms and halls are booked for the next year's teaching and examinations.

For the second year 'A' Level students, thirty-three per cent of their examination is over. 'Debriefing' rather than evaluation needs to take place in a meeting of the class. Targets must be set for the students with regard to their written examination.

Summer Term

Second year students should be reminded of the examination timetable. The revision timetable should be devised and understood fully.

Revision essays are written, revision of set texts is undertaken, 'unseen' practice is given to the second year students. First year students have full use of the practice halls in working on their set texts. During the second half of the term, they may lose the use of the school hall to examination use. The timetable of hall use needs to be explained carefully to the first year students, so that no useful time is lost.

Examination at 'A' Level
Meeting of students and team teachers. If appropriate, a questionnaire may be offered to the students to obtain any valuable points for review by the staff. Evaluation of the course by all involved, including parents.

See also 'Summer Term' above.

Summer Recess

Evaluation of results by teaching staff
Continuing 'customer service' through discussion with individual students as they return to school, regarding their results and their career.

See also 'Summer Recess' above.

Nothing left to do but retire or return to the beginning of the calendar.

Note: This calendar is adaptable to any school. Each school needs to devise a calendar. Each school needs to fill in dates and to modfity the calendar each year.

Chapter 10

The Listening School: Sixth Formers and Staff as Customers of Each Other

Robert Whatmough

Introduction

Drawing on aspects of the thinking behind Total Quality Management and a number of its techniques, a quality improvement project focusing on aspects of sixth form provision is under way at my school. The following account describes preparatory work completed in the summer term of 1993, looks briefly at initial implementation at the start of the school year 1993–4, and anticipates the direction in which future developments may lie.

In the course of the chapter, I hope also to outline some difficulties with TQM as applied to schools and to suggest some possible ways forward.

Total Quality Management – A Rational Response

'Just do it'?

Of course, John West-Burnham's *Managing Quality in Schools* (1992) ends, not with a question mark, but with an exclamation (p.146):

> Summary
> – Plan, act, review.
> Action
> – 'Just do it!'

His work is essentially a call to action rather than reflection. TQM is about *doing something* in the battle for excellence, not spending too much time, as teams in schools are prone to do, 'debating issues and principles' when energy should be directed towards 'solving problems, formulating solutions and developing a commitment to action'

(West-Burnham, 1992, p.120).

The enthusiasm of TQM advocates, when supported by much practical advice, has considerable appeal to the practising teacher. However, reservations are prompted by some of the principal ideas put forward.

Customer-defined Quality

The most problematic area of TQM is the definition of quality itself. On this key matter, most proponents uphold a common theme: quality is defined by the customer. A helpful illustration of this idea in practice, as it affects manufacturing industry, is provided in the Department for Enterprise booklet on TQM and effective leadership (DTI, 1992a). The director of manufacturing for Black and Decker UK (Robin Mair) points out that a prospective customer will shake a power drill to see if it rattles. If it does, s/he will not buy it. The rattle may not affect the tool's function, but it determines the choice between one company's product and another's. In Mair's words: 'Customer perception is the only reality' (DTI, 1992a, p.21).

Mair's conclusion is fraught with difficulty. While a lost sale is a lost sale, the quality of an electrical product does not *solely* reside in the customer's view of it. Consider the health and safety implications of using an inherently dangerous tool: a rattling drill which does not harm its user is of higher quality than one which, though aurally perfect, is shoddily made and liable to cause the user to receive an electric shock. The quality of the drill, in this sense, lies within the production process and the product, and needs to be considered by the supplier *regardless of whether customers individually or collectively demand it or not.* Indeed, Black and Decker would no doubt agree that there are some customers who need protecting from themselves.

TQM and Education – A Blind Alley?

The more fitting notion of customers as partners, not final arbiters, in the definition of quality is developed by Øvretveit (1992) in his work on the National Health Service. Øvretveit recognizes the fallibility of customers or clients (which is not to deny the fallibility of professionals) and starts from an important distinction between 'wants' and 'needs':

> We often think of a quality service as one which gives us what we want – that quality is customer satisfaction. Quality in this book means some-

thing different. It means a service which gives people what they need, as well as what they want, and does so at lowest cost (Øvretveit, 1992, p.1).

He suggests ways in which some things are too important, complex or problematic to leave to customer choice alone:

> We cannot define quality only in terms of client satisfaction and expressed demand. The clients of the health service may not know what they need, or may ask for treatments that really are inappropriate or harmful (Øvretveit, 1992, p.5).

The implications of this for the education service are fairly obvious but need to be stated explicitly because they are so much out of fashion. While the parental dictum, 'I know what's best for my child' is true in many situations, it is arguably not so in others. Are we content, for example, to agree that schools should provide a computer-free curriculum for the children of parents belonging to religious groups who regard such technology as, quite literally, the work of the devil? In a less extreme form, are we to collude with parents who wish to act on the belief that 'grammar school' is synonymous with 'good school', often regardless of their child's ability? Or, if pupils are also customers, do we wish to return to the days when 14-year old girls would commonly express their preferences by dropping all contact with chemical and physical sciences?

Principles of curriculum entitlement and the moral imperative to give due regard to all the stakeholders in education would suggest that basing provision on customer choice alone is wrong.

TQM and Education – The Way Forward

However, problems with the definition of quality in TQM do not mean that there is nothing of value in its spirit and practice. Only the fundamentalist believer insists on the necessity of accepting the whole package. It is fair to doubt West-Burnham's judgement that 'piecemeal involvement is doomed' (1992, p.136). Calling into question accepted wisdom concerning the supposed resurrection of quality does not preclude involvement in its aftermath.

Sixth Formers and Staff as Customers of Each Other

Context

Chapter School is situated in the small town of Strood in Kent. It is a girls' secondary school with a roll of just under 900. Formally designated a 'high school', it has a non-selective intake and operates in an area where most high-ability pupils attend grammar schools. The school has, however, a well-established sixth form (including a small number of male students) and offers a full range of courses: A Levels, GCSEs, BTEC and GNVQ. In August 1993, as a result of a wholesale reorganization of education in the area, the school moved site to refurbished premises.

Quality Improvement – The Challenge

A combination of negative and positive factors prompted a review of aspects of sixth form provision:

- *Staff concerns* – meetings at senior and middle management level recognized the value of recent curricular innovation aimed at ensuring a closer match between the individual student and her/his course. However, concerns were identified about such matters as student motivation and attendance.
- *Preparation for new site* – in conjunction with the whole staff, concentrated attention was given to the most appropriate ways of preparing students for the opportunities contained within the facilities on our future site. There was a determination to build in quality right from the start, not attempt to control for it later.
- *Mission statement* – the governors' mission statement, formulated at the height of the debate over the school's future, is a forceful expression of beliefs and intent. No doubt in common with many such statements, it articulates values which are perceived to be essential and unchanging while holding out the promise of an invigorating future.

There is, however, awareness among both governors and senior staff that, if an institution aspires to quality, 'It must innovate and drive ahead to achieve the vision contained in the mission statement' (Sallis, 1993, p.81). The quality improvement project described here may be thought of as one step towards realization of the governors' vision.

Implementation

The first stages of the project sought to ascertain in a more objective and thorough manner the perceptions of those involved in the current situation, and to develop a model of quality management which was both theoretically defensible and, in terms of moving things on, supportive of staff effort and morale.

Developing a Working Definition of Quality

Quality, in terms of sixth form provision, is seen by the informal quality circle we formed to be essentially the outcome of the interface between two often contiguous, occasionally conflicting, dimensions:

- client view of quality
- professional view of quality.

Sixth form students and staff are seen, within the framework adopted, as customers of each other.

Client View of Quality

In key respects, it is possible to view sixth form students as customers or clients of the service which the school provides to a degree which is not the case for younger pupils:

- there is no legal obligation on 16+ students to attend any form of education;
- schools must compete with colleges to attract their customers;
- students are as free to leave an institution as they are to join it;
- 16+ students are more independent from their parents and are thus more readily seen as primary customers.

In common with health service customers (Øvretveit, 1992), students are likely to view the service they have chosen with a mixture of conscious expectations and unconscious assumptions. They may be disillusioned as a result of the disparity between an idealized view of the sixth form and the reality they find as they embark on their courses. They may express a constant wish 'to be treated as adults' but have a simplistic view of what that might entail in practice.

They are the best, indeed the only, people to ask about what it is like to be on the receiving end of experiences provided by the school. From the point of view of both institutional survival and improvement, students' own definitions of quality have to be a decisive influence in the development of 16+ provision.

Professional Quality

In his discussion of the monitoring of client satisfaction, Thomson (1989) suggests that belief in the value of listening to students' views does not entail automatically accepting them. Rather, quality monitoring allows schools to review their activities taking a student-centred perspective. The responsible school manager will then be in the position of being '...well informed and able to interpret the information available – to accept it or reject it' (Thomson, 1989, p.188).

Thomson's work clearly proceeds along the line of identifying a core of issues about which professional and student views can agree. However, the possibility of the professional view overriding the clients' has to be kept in reserve.

Sixth Formers and Staff in the Quality Chain

West-Burnham (1992) illustrates the important TQM idea of a 'quality chain' by means of the example of the organization of a school trip. The trip will not be successful unless all participants in the chain are identified, understand their roles and accept responsibility for performing them to the satisfaction of everyone else. The implications of this model are that, 'Everyone is a supplier and a customer. There are equal responsibilities on suppliers and customers' (p.29).

Extending these ideas to the relationship between teachers and sixth form students has so far proved to be a liberating experience. Although the ideas are not in themselves strikingly new – 'you scratch my back and I'll scratch yours' would be inappropriate in tone but not entirely dissimilar in effect – the reinterpretation of the notion of mutual reciprocity in terms of service given and received has permitted the articulation of wants, needs and expectations on all sides. The way has been opened for a more explicitly defined relationship between students and staff and greater recognition of the ways in which students themselves are 'producers' in terms of the success or otherwise of a course.

Øvretveit (1992) holds out the prospect of a situation 'where clients' expectations are frequently discussed and an implicit "service contract" is "negotiated" with each client' (p.40). In the context of a school and the extended contact between service provider and client, such a contract can be explicit and part of the educative process itself.

Pastoral Team Meeting

A special meeting of the Year 12 and 13 tutors, together with the head of sixth form discussed the current situation and possible ways forward. Specific outcomes included:

- a decision to develop a school-student partnership agreement, including a clear statement of expectations concerning attendance;

- modification of the induction programme for new sixth form students to include attention to assertiveness skills as a means of facilitating their contribution to both the formulation and implementation of the partnership agreement;
- a decision to survey existing Year 12 students to discover their perceptions of the strengths and weaknesses of the sixth form (and to act as a check on our subjective impressions of their views).

Student Participation in Quality Improvement

Surprisingly, writers on TQM in schools frequently make only passing reference to the integration of pupils themselves into the process of quality improvement.

Having decided to follow the TQM route of discovering the customers' views of their needs and their response to the school's provision, it seemed appropriate to involve a small but representative group of Year 12 students in the formulation of a questionnaire and analysis of its results. Unfortunately, the questionnaire was undertaken at a point in the summer term when students were already starting to 'disappear' into study leave or post-assessment employment. As a result, while it was possible to ensure that all Year 12 students received a copy, in the end only 34 out of a possible 86 questionnaires were returned. This low rate significantly reduced the value of the exercise, while nevertheless confirming the importance of measuring student satisfaction.

It should, perhaps, be added that this year a survey of the current Year 12 has been undertaken at a point in the school year where it is possible to do something about any problems which are identified.

Responses

The questions asked and students' responses are set out in Figure 10.1.

CHAPTER SCHOOL

SIXTH FORM SURVEY

The aim of this survey is to find out what you think and feel about the sixth form as a result of your personal experience of Year 12.

The survey is confidential. We ask you to answer the questions carefully. Space is provided for you to add extra comments if you wish. Please avoid criticism of individual students or staff.

The results of the survey will be carefully analysed. They will be used to help plan for the future.

Thank you for your help.

May 1993

A. COURSE

Please circle the number which shows best how far you agree or disagree with each statement.

	Strongly Disagree	Disagree	Neither Agree nor Disgree	Agree	Strongly Agree
1. The written information available about sixth form courses was helpful.	6	29	18	41	6
2. I received good advice about my choice of subjects or course from teachers	6	15	44	29	6
3. The range of subjects and courses on offer met my needs.	3	9	20	56	12
4. I chose my subjects or course because of pressure from other people, eg parents or teachers	35	35	18	12	0
5. I chose my subjects or course because they were what I wanted to do.	0	3	27	41	29
6. Overall, I have found my subjects or course interesting.	0	3	15	70	12
7. I think my subjects or course will help me in the future to get a job.	0	6	15	44	35
8. Overall, I am pleased with my Year 12 subjects or course.	3	9	15	58	15

Please add extra comments if you wish:

9. I have been following (please circle):
   NVQ
   BTEC
   GCSEs
   GCSEs + A LEVELS

B. WORK

Please tell us about the work in class, assignments, projects and other work involved in your course.

	Strongly Disagree	Disagree	Neither Agree nor Disgree	Agree	Strongly Agree
1. Overall, I have enjoyed my lessons this year.	3	3	29	53	12
2. Work at home, e.g. on assignments, has been an important feature of my course.	0	3	17	65	15
3. Help has been readily available from my teachers.	3	9	32	41	15
4. I have developed important skills (things I can do) this year.	0	12	26	41	21
5. My work has helped me to grow in confidence.	3	15	32	26	24
6. I have been able to find a quiet place in school in which to work.	12	18	26	35	9
7. The library has been a good place in which to work.	3	24	21	35	17
8. Deadlines should be kept to more strictly by teachers.	3	9	29	27	32
9. I found Work Experience in Year 12 interesting and helpful	14	10	30	23	23

10. Overall, the amount of work has been for me

too much	18
about right	79
too little	3

11. Overall, the level of work has been for me

too difficult	0
about right	100
too easy	0

Please add extra comments if you wish:

C. RELATIONSHIPS

	Strongly Disagree	Disagree	Neither Agree nor Disgree	Agree	Strongly Agree
1. Year 12 students have been supportive of each other.	3	0	15	59	23
2. There has been a good relationship between Years 12 and 13.	12	12	38	32	6
3. Younger pupils respect the sixth form.	12	35	32	18	3
4. The sixth form respect younger pupils	3	15	41	35	6
5. I have a good, working relationship with my teachers.	3	9	18	64	6
6. My relationship with teachers has improved since Year 11.	6	9	15	61	9
7. I feel that I can approach staff about difficulties with my work.	3	6	20	56	15
8. I feel that I can approach staff if I have a personal problem.	15	29	35	18	3
9. Years 12 + 13 sharing common room with help create unity in the Sixth Form.	29	9	29	18	15

D. COMMON ROOM

	Strongly Disagree	Disagree	Neither Agree nor Disgree	Agree	Strongly Agree
1. The atmosphere in the common room has been enjoyable.	0	0	15	47	38
2. The facilities in the common room need improvement.	0	0	3	21	76
3. Improved facilities would lead to greater care by students.	0	0	15	32	53

E. SUMMARY

1. I would recommend the sixth
   form to a friend.   YES/NO
                        79/21

Suggestions for an improved sixth form on the new site:

1.

2.

3.

4.

5.

Figure 10.1 Sixth form questionnaire

Detailed interpretation of the results is of considerable interest within the institution. For example, how should we respond to the fact that 79 per cent of students ticked 'yes' to the acid test question: 'I would recommend the sixth form to a friend'? The temptation is to be pleased by the high figure. However, the 21 per cent who responded 'no' were seven individuals who may well regret their decision to stay on at school. This is a matter for concern in itself and also because their disenchantment may be communicated to other actual or prospective students.

Dilemmas

Some of the free-written comments highlighted the dilemmas in the development of a TQM-related approach in schools. The first underlines the difficulty of accepting a purely customer-oriented approach. The following impassioned outburst is a vivid reminder of how the customer will measure the school's promises against reality. However, would it be professional or wise to consent to the student's prescription for herself and her teachers?

> 'I chose to come back. If I do not hand in any work, that's my choice. I know how it will affect me in the long run. Stick to your guns and treat us like adults like you say you are going to do and stop nagging!'

The second concerns comments made about individual staff. In spite of being requested not to criticize individual students or teachers, two students wrote strong condemnations of members of staff. One set of these comments was clearly and fully reasoned and expressed regret at the respondent's need to override the request which had been made.

For the moment, I have explained to the students who remain from the original group that I have replaced these respondents' forms with photocopies which have the personal criticisms blanked out. In the longer term, a more adequate response will be to build into the sixth form tutor programme further clear and explicit opportunities to articulate concerns before they become insurmountable obstacles.

Whatever procedure is adopted, the possibility will always remain that, if invited to give their own views, students may well elect to express them in a manner which is oblivious to professional etiquette.

Update

How are the various strands identified in the project coming together in a manner which is enhancing the quality of sixth form provision? The following has happened or is about to happen in the next term or so:

- all Year 12 students experienced a full day's induction which was modified as a result of the analysis of our current situation to include work on relationships with other years and on the development of assertiveness skills;
- the new common room has been laid out in a manner reflecting discussions held with prospective students in the summer term;
- a four-week trial period was used to allow students and staff time to show ways in which they will meet each other's needs;
- a formal partnership agreement has been drawn up, which will be binding on both sides and embodies the notion of students and staff as customers of each other;
- a mid-year review has been implemented, which will lead to further action to enhance the quality of provision.

Overall, the prospects for continuous quality improvement look good even if the first term with new students and initial difficulties with rooms and buildings reminded us that the perfection of zero defects may be a long way off.

Conclusion

There is nothing like a kick in the professional rectum to send one back to the barricades. Edward Pearce, writing in *The Guardian,* condemns teachers for clinging on to what he sees as an outmoded view of professionalism,

> Teachers are a producer group. Like other producer groups with a status quo which asks few questions of them, they want that status quo left intact. But frankly, why should the consumers want it? (Pearce, 1993).

Much as one may object to the tone of the article, it articulates the spirit of accountability and consumer-responsiveness which underpins the philosophy of TQM. It catches the negative spirit of the times in portraying professional groups as self-serving and dismissing their claims to be performing honourable public service as whitewash.

I have tried in my account of work in progress to redefine the supplier-consumer relationship in education as essentially one of partnership, with the demands of professional quality as a last resort overriding consumer perceptions where conflict cannot be avoided. I recognize that this is a compromise that cannot be accommodated within pure TQM. However, it does go some way towards professional humility which hints at 'the possibility of improvement, of more being got out of education or given to children' (Pearce, 1993). It supports the notion of a dynamic of continuous improvement, and recognizes that our schools may never be as good as we can make them.

Chapter 11

Investors in People in a College of Further Education

Heather Speller

The further education sector has found itself in the front line of curriculum and management change. Quality management development within educational institutions is challenging traditional structures and methods. Incorporation has highlighted the need for new management skills that provide empowerment to staff backed by a sound strategy, structure and systems that enable the institution to progress. South Kent College is using the Investors in People standards to support their quest for continuous improvement. This chapter gives an account of experiences gained whilst progressing implementation.

Background

South Kent College is in Eurotunnel country! The college has needed to respond as major developments in the local economic infrastructure impact on traditional employment areas and in turn on the unemployment on the coast. The college is on three sites with as many campus cultures. It has nearly 600 staff, teaching and non-teaching: 356 full-time and 235 part-time. Student numbers exceed 3,600 full-time equivalents although a high percentage of these are part-time students. Programmes taught are in line with normal FE provision, i.e. craft and vocational, NVQs and GNVQs, special learning difficulties and disabilities, GCSE O and A level, degree access, and a smattering of degree provision. The college structure could be explained as 'pseudo-matrix', having six departments.

On 1 April 1993 the college became a corporate body and part of the sector coordinated by the Further Education Funding Council (FEFC). This freedom from LEAs has brought a mixed bag of changes to the sector, many of which are focused around quality assurance-related issues. In March 1993 the college committed itself to attaining the Investors in People standard.

The National Standard

The national standard for effective investment in people is based upon a core theme which hinges on a staff development/training plan enabling the organization to secure corporate goals. In other words the organization needs to identify a framework for planning and assessing investment in employees' abilities.

The standard is structured around four main principles, namely those associated with *commitment,* from top management to invest in people to achieve business goals; *planning* how skills of individuals and teams are to be developed to achieve organizational goals; *action* to develop and use necessary skills in a well-defined and continuing programme; and mechanisms that *evaluate* progress towards goals, value achieved and future needs.

The four principles have a total of 26 associated indicators against which an organization can measure itself and be assessed and attain the standard. The process for achieving the standard is supported by the local Training and Enterprise Councils (TECs) who provide information and financial support (although the funding levels available do vary from region to region). Achieving the standard can be broken down into four main phases:

- Reviewing current practice against the standard in terms of a 'health check' diagnostic instrument. (This can often involve a questionnaire, or interview schedule, targeted at specific whole sections or the whole organization).
- Producing an action plan, (to plug the gaps highlighted in the diagnostic health check phase) indicating appropriate action to be taken, and making a formal commitment to pursue the standard.
- The implementation phase, when actions highlighted in the action plan are put into practice, and the whole approach is brought up to a level that meets the requirements of the standard. Supporting documentary evidence is produced.
- The final phase of assessment and recognition requires an organization to produce a portfolio of evidence, (we were told 'a maximum of 60 pages, no "forklift truck jobs": this is not a bureaucratic exercise'). A major aspect of assessment is the

'walk about' inspection by the external assessor appointed via the TEC, during which a cross-section of staff are interviewed. The responses and perceptions of these staff are critical in formulating the assessor's recommendations. Successful institutions are allowed to display the Investors in People laurel leaf logo, until the next assessment three years later.

Investors in People in a Broader Context

The Investors in People standard was launched by the Confederation of British Industry (CBI) at their annual conference in 1991. Introductory development had been led by the National Training Task Force in partnership with the TECs and business through the CBI, the Association of British Chambers of Commerce (ABCC), the Institute of Personnel Management (IPM) and others. The first 28 companies to attain the standard were recognized in the autumn of 1992. These included well-known names such as Nissan, Pirelli and Unilever. By early 1994 more than 575 recognitions and 6,000 commitments were recorded, including seven FE colleges and four schools. Recognitions have continued, but not it seems in line with the government's wishes to fulfil the National Education and Training Targets for Lifetime Learning, set at half of all organizations with more than 200 employees achieving the standard by 1996.

The rationale for the introduction of the Investors in People standard is clear enough; in the late 1980s industry and commerce were spending in excess of £20 billion on training (Taylor, 1991) but most of this was not strategically planned. Money spent on training was regarded as a 'cost' rather than an 'investment'. The IPM report, *Quality: People Management Matters* (1993) certainly indicated little shift in this view. The Institute's commissioning of a study on 'the human resource dimension of quality management' gives guidance to its members on the 'challenges posed for people management' (Marchington et al., 1993). Mostly training was not strategically planned or evaluated and it certainly was not always available to all employees. The launch of the Investors standard and the Employment Department's support are significant, the government having backed the BS 5750/ISO 9000 management systems approach as a starting point to quality management (Oakland, 1989) through the Department of Trade and Industry's 'Into the 90s Initiative'. It seemed that such initiatives overlooked the more holistic requirements of 'continuous improvement', 'Kaizen', promoted in Total Quality Management (TQM) (Hutchins, 1992).

Subsequently, as the applicability of quality management systems within a broader range of contexts emerged, organizational culture and Human Resource Management (HRM) became recognized as more significant (Oakland, 1992) in an holistic approach to TQM. Quality developments in Japan and America promoted such an approach; for example the US government-backed Malcolm Baldridge National Quality Award gives a considerable weighting to effective human resource utilization. The United Kingdom's shortfall was due to a distinct 'focus on "hard" systems type initiatives and their failure to pay sufficient attention to the people elements in the drive for continuous improvement' (Wilkinson *et al.,* 1992). Initiatives to address this balance include the setting up of the European Foundation for Quality Management (EFQM) in 1991 and the European Quality Award and the launch by Michael Heseltine and the DTI, with the British Quality Foundation, of the British Quality Award in February 1994. These certainly bear out a recognition of a far more rounded approach. Allen Sheppard, chairman and chief executive of Grand Metropolitan plc and former chairman of the National Training Task Force saw the links, and commented encouragingly on the publication of BSI's advisory TQM guidelines (BS 7850). He drew attention to the relevance of Investors in People for any employer seeking to introduce TQM: 'People are at the heart of quality management and Investors in People provides a framework for the effective involvement and development of people at work' (Sheppard, 1992).

We must recognize that the UK 'disease' of poor investment in people is important. We need to be concerned with IIP as a nation because we do need a more highly skilled and flexible workforce who feel valued. If we are to compete internationally there is a need to reduce labour turnover and take advantage of other positive business benefits, which IIP can promote – 'less work in progress, shorter lead in times, – less scrap, and rejections, – less customer complaints. All these = competitive advantage and therefore an improved bottom line' (Taylor, 1991).

Applicability of the Standard to Education

Initially, the BS 5750/ISO 9000 management systems approach to quality management was promoted as applicable to all aspects of commerce, industry and the public sector. Significantly, service sector organizations in particular presented problems when introducing such approaches. This was to a large degree the result of failure by organizations to pay sufficient attention to 'people elements' in the race for quality improvement (Wilkinson *et al.*, 1992). A common feature identified when implementing management systems was problems concerned with reviewing and changing attitudes of employees and organizational culture. This was particularly so in the public sector service organizations, like the health service, local government and education. Here the notion of market forces and competitiveness has emerged only recently in response to government policy. An emphasis on market forces, being customer focused, defining and measuring quality, is particularly problematic. Moving such structures from an administrative to a management culture presented huge problems that in the main are yet to be addressed. The Investors in People standard appeals and is totally compatible with the ethos of education. This was reinforced when Baroness Blatch addressed the Investors in People in Education CBI Conference on 4 December 1992, mentioning, as though it were quite obviously the right thing to do, that the DFE were committed to achieving the standard.

Investors in People as an approach probably presents the most realistic way to address the quality management challenges the FE sector currently faces. The enlightened have long recognized that training and development are essential for academic staff and the introduction of appraisal schemes reflects these concerns. Once the language of the standard is translated into an FE context, colleges that have investigated the standard have quickly realized that they already undertake most of the activities that are required to be recognized as an 'Investor in People', and that commitment to the standard can provide them with a highly effective framework for a whole-staff training and development policy. The process revolves around the idea that there is a planning cycle within all colleges. The college writes a business development plan which has an agreed vision; the vision is conveyed to the whole organization, members of which must be able to have an input into planning and the execution of the plan, thus supporting a unanimity of purpose across the structure. The organizational strategy is open to change/adaptation at any time and is concerned with the personal development of individuals alongside the team, department and the overall organization. The process, if used correctly, could embody the principle of ownership and empowerment. The TEC's requirements of Work Related Further Education (WRFE) courses and of TEC Quality Supplier Management (TQSM) are wholly compatible with IIP. The White Paper, *Education and Training in the 21st Century* (DES, 1991b), flagged the significance of TQM and BS 5750 to the FE sector; IIP as an approach is compatible with both of these. Furthermore, the FEFC circulars 92/01, 92/11, 92/18, and 94/01 particularly highlighted the significance of strategic planning. The links with the standard are critical. College strategic plans started off very weakly in the late 1980s but have sharpened up in response to the changes thrust upon the sector. IIP applied within these national, local and institutional contexts underlines the necessity of a maintained staff development budget, whilst the logo signals recognized 'good practice' – a useful marketing tool.

Why South Kent College opted for the 'Laurel Leaf Logo'

Prior to the college's commitment to the national standard, there was a history of staff development practice, initiated in 1984, followed by a college-wide annual range of activities known as 'Frontline'. The Frontline programme also supported individual staff through a range of external programmes, many of them leading to qualifications, or credit accumulation, others providing updating, etc. In recognition of the good practice that was established, and the changing curricular needs, a full cross-college department known as Staff and Curriculum Development was created. The new department flourished and as it grew it added, amongst others, units of staff development, teacher training and quality assurance. From this base in the late 1980s and early 1990s quality assurance management methods were researched, as were curriculum quality issues, all of these feeding into a cross-college strategy that tried to anticipate the changing demands the sector was experiencing. Appraisal had been approached in much the same way, and the research consultation and supporting staff development had achieved a professionally acceptable model. We had invested in a day's training for all appraisers and appraisees, thus promoting the 'drive out fear' philosophy (number eight of Deming's [1988] 14 points). Ben Thomason, the principal, was keen that he should be appraised first, and then a cascade proceeded through the senior management team and so on down through the departments. He was known for fully supporting the notion of an 'open management' philosophy for valuing and empowering individuals. The college strategic plans produced for each of the four years prior to embarking upon IIP had improved, each year becoming more streamlined and presented in a more structured way.

The college quality assurance framework was designed in 1990 to enable all practitioners to conduct and participate in a programme review activity which included a range of evidence from customer/ student survey responses. These fed into team, departmental and college planning processes and initially produced some quite notice- able developments in terms of visible resourcing, i.e. crèche, coffee shop, etc. The college quality assurance policy stated: 'South Kent College aims to provide for its students, customers and the commu- nity, excellent education, training and services. Continuous improve- ment will become a permanent feature'. The strategy was to be managed in four dimensions that enable the development of the whole South Kent College experience:

1. the clientele;
2. the curriculum;
3. the management;
4. the personnel.

Attention to 'the clientele' and 'the curriculum' has been explicit and forceful, but some internal processes concerned with communi- cation and staff care and development (dimensions 3 and 4) need further attention to match the college's quality assurance policy – and IIP.

Working towards IIP

During the summer of 1992 Kent TEC approached the college with a view to encouraging participation in the IIP initiative. The senior management team and governors were made aware of the initiative and gave it their support. A target for achieving the standard was identified in the three-year plan. By January 1993 diagnostic devel- opments were well under way. It had been decided to survey the senior management team with a diagnostic instrument, developed from the original Investors 'Tool kit' from the Further Education Staff College at Coombe Lodge, Bristol. This was rewritten in 'South-Kent-College-speak', and subsequently distributed to all members of staff on the college payroll. The managers' survey was produced using the same formulae and circulated to the senior management team. The response rates for the surveys were 33 per cent from the staff survey and 90 per cent from management. The response revealed something about the effectiveness of the internal communications processes, and about the status accorded the task by the management. These returns were used to form a basis for the college action plan. It was interesting that the two surveys sometimes produced contradictory responses, although there was general agreement on many issues. Also, some of the indicators in the diagnostic surveys were impossible to correlate, making the subsequent drawing up of the action plan document a tedious exercise. Having worked hard at producing the action plan and project targets, we had originally felt quite pleased with our documents, but then began to realize that a wider, more prolonged consultative stage may well have been useful.

The projected action plan and accompanying letter of commitment to Kent TEC resulted in an in-house commitment launch in the presence of Kent TEC's chief executive and college's senior management. All staff were invited to attend but participation was not high, due in part to the launch being held at the Folkestone site, at the end of the afternoon and during a normal teaching week. Our commitment was dated 1 April 1993, the day the FE sector officially stood away from the LEA. At that time we had not anticipated the changes and demands the new status would impose on the college. All the while we were increasingly aware of our original anticipated assessment target date of June 1994.

Some very positive progress was made during the summer of 1993. We raised the profile of the IIP initiative with a monthly newsletter, reviewed internal and external marketing practices in line with the ethos of the standard, and delivered in-house training to departments on the standard and its applicability. The most beneficial sessions linked IIP, our in-house quality improvement programme via a 'student entitlement' curriculum policy initiative, and departmental planning. The summer term ended, and a budget deficit became the focus of a number of worries. There was a freeze on new appointments and staff morale dipped. The realization slowly dawned that a number of albeit voluntary redundancies would be required, with subsequent changes resulting probably in a restructuring. All this challenged the themes in IIP, which was concerned with developing and valuing individuals. Staff felt worried, pressurized with the significant curricular challenges, and undervalued. Values and morale were, it seemed to some, coloured by the budget-led decisions that were beginning to influence every action that was taken. The staff were not at all relaxed or happy. Just as a year previously when we surveyed the staff, the early New Year seemed a grey and doubtful time to start any new initiative. Doubts, fears about changes, and challenges loomed up inexplicably, leading to a hiatus between traditional roles and the complex developments the new changes we were experiencing would make. It seemed to be almost unimaginable, but the goodwill and the professional values and judgements that we had come to rely upon in the past were replaced with comments about burdens, worries and a lack of resources. There was a distinct vacuum where we would ordinarily have expected energy and support. The staff were tired and some departments carried heavy overtime workloads. It was difficult trying to inspire individuals to help themselves and to plan and use staff development in a meaningful way whilst we were wondering what other changes were going to be on our agendas.

Nevertheless, cynicism, like many other attitudinal states, has its day, and the project coordinators found themselves looking to the future. A New Year, a new start. The anticipated assessment schedule for IIP was dropped back and the plan progressed at a more realistic pace. The senior managers had been briefed on a number of occasions regarding the initiative. Their workload with all the other changes could distract from the IIP initiative; they would need plenty of reminders. 'Keep on their shoulders', we were advised by John Fosdyke at Kent TEC.

The next target group was to be the appraisers, the middle managers. The IIP team had to change its attitudes and practices with regard to training and evaluation, and establish more coherent and structured arrangements. A number of half-day workshops were set up, which have proved useful and certainly have enabled a more open discussion. The rescheduled action plan has had to be flexible. Pressure of work at peak time (for example, enrolments) has to be taken into consideration, as does the 'down time' during holidays when staff are not in, but at these times major administrative tasks and preparation can be moved forward.

Currently our plans are on schedule: we are finding our previous experiences particularly useful. Looking back, April 1993 may not have been the best time to commence the initiative. When is a good time? There is still a long way to go and we cannot pretend that we will not have some challenges ahead. IIP can not be viewed as a quick fix or a 'sheep dip' initiative in terms of awareness raising. The promulgation of a business-like approach to HRM and the establishment of an audit trail will make sure we use our most valuable asset, our staff, effectively. Such an appraisal also requires us to look at our communications processes and improve them. IIP at South Kent is a positive development for staff 'entitlement', and it is the way we have chosen to initiate continual improvement.

Chapter 12

BS 5750 and on to TQM in a College of Further Education: Laughing, Crying and Loving

Les Franklin

Introduction

There has developed throughout the 1980s a school of theorists seeking to understand the process and pace of industrial change. Deming (1982), Peters (1989), Peters and Austin (1985), Peters and Waterman (1982) and Kanter (1990) have all attempted to document and analyse the ways that adaptive organizations have responded to an increasingly competitive and changing environment. Peters, for instance, believes that greater competition results in successful organizations restructuring both organizational arrangements and operating methods to remain competitive. Bound up within the quickening pace of change and competition has been the emergence of quality as an issue. As markets and market share have come under attack (or suffered erosion) so organizations have sought to safeguard their existing position, or penetrate new markets, by adopting a quality philosophy. The effect nationally of increasing competition has been the relative decline of the industrial base and accompanying high levels of unemployment. The upshot of all of this for Further Education (FE) has been a deterioration of its traditional market. Consequently, FE has undergone some dramatic changes in the last decade with a swing away from a narrow correspondence with the needs of industry through the 'new FE' to, for some, a current obsession with quality.

East Birmingham College, with a tradition of serving the heartland of manufacturing, has suffered more than most from continued economic decline. The result has been that radical changes have taken place in the College's market and, to better accommodate new customers, internal organization. Accompanying the changes has been the emergence of quality as a major concern.

Beginning by acknowledging the synonymity between quality and equality, and accompanied by many of the expansive beliefs embodied in the Total Quality Management (TQM) movement, the College has moved on to the introduction of the tight procedural controls of BS 5750. This step became necessary, in part, to impose and recapture organizational control and aid conformance, by developing systematic quality assurance. However, a further factor influencing the decision was a growing demand from surviving industry that the College integrate with its quality procedures.

The College's inclusion on the BS 5750 register in 1992 is believed by senior managers to be the platform to continue a progressive, controlled, movement into TQM. However, maintaining the quality assurance system carries within it the danger of the system being seen as an end in itself. A further negative, attitudinal factor, is the feeling amongst some staff that the achievement of BS 5750 certification was the end of the journey rather than a beginning.

Change of Mission

For Venables (1967) East Birmingham College was so typical of FE's correspondence with industry that she used the College as the centre-piece of her research. This relationship with industry reached its peak in 1970 with the College achieving over one million student-hours for the year. If any doubt was harboured about the primacy of industry to the then mission of the College, the steady decline through the 1970s of both industry and students is a sharp reminder. By the late 1970s there was a strong case to be made for closure of the College. However, a change of mission not only reversed the trend but by the 1990s student-hours far exceeded the previous high-water mark.

The mission change was to provide for the 'new FE'. This theme, founded as it is on the premise that all of the community should be encouraged to see the college as providing for its needs, meant that a supporting infrastructure of equal opportunity policies and student services became necessary. The strategy was given added importance by the College's location and a need to have policies addressing the deprivation of the inner city, with a particular emphasis on the needs of ethnic minorities.

As policies became transformed into practice, and staff capable of assisting such a transformation were introduced, the culture of the College took on a 'softer', more humanistic focus. Nevertheless, a substantial amount of industry-related work remained, creating something of a contradiction. This contradiction manifested itself in the way that quality came to symbolize links with both the community and industry.

Gleeson and Mardle (1980) have acknowledged that technical teachers within FE have a tendency to recreate and stress correspondence with industry. In grounding their reality and cultural identity in the world of work, anything at odds with this is perceived to be 'unreal' and meaningless. The move to stronger links with the community and a 'softer' College orientation apparently challenged this self-perception. However, potential resistance to the new mission was weakened by the steady, inexorable, decline of local industry and the consequent haemorrhaging of teaching posts. Nevertheless, the decision, in 1990, to pave the way to BS 5750 certification, synonymous as the standard is with industry, might have been interpreted by the remaining technical teachers as a signal that the College's former mission was about to reassert itself.

Any potential conflict over direction was overcome by senior managers blending the old and the new missions of the College together and fostering the belief that the College was in a unique position to act as a 'broker' for the community by creating access to opportunity, including employment with the companies the College served. Accordingly, it was necessary for the College to have simultaneously a 'soft' and a 'hard' focus to quality, with involvement with companies or community regarded as part of the same mission.

Current use of the term 'quality' recognizes both a narrow definition: 'fitness for purpose' (Caplan 1989, p.3), emanating from manufacturing, and a much broader, wide-ranging version, founded on 'quality judged as the customer perceives it' (Peters, 1989, p.82). Allied to the second, broader version are deeper implications; Peters argues that it is akin to a philosophical/moral position. It is this broader, richer version that first shaped the College's approach to quality and led the College towards inner-city initiatives.

Quality and the Community

The richer 'soft' interpretation of quality is best understood as representative of the humanistic – people first – elements contained within the TQM movement. For the College this has included 'closeness' to the customer. This strategy, an essential element in terms of 'quality' as defined by Peters, has manifested itself in a policy of physically taking the College to the community, with the result that curriculum programme areas now deliver 20 per cent of their total programme in the inner city at centres established for the purpose. Further reinforcement has come from adopting a strong equal opportunities programme, including target setting.

A letter to staff, from the College's principal, outlines the reasons for the move to the inner city:

To: All Staff
From: Tony Henry
Date: 24 April 1991

Please find attached a copy of a letter I sent to the Chair of Governors yesterday, which I feel explains WHY we are doing it.

Dear Chair of Governors,

Deprivation and East Birmingham College

As it is St George's Day and as I was not successful in getting a free British Airways flight I thought that I may as well write to you about something. You may know that I am delivering a paper towards the end of next week at a T.E.C. Quality conference. In preparing for that event I have found out some very illuminating things about East Birmingham which I am sure will be of interest to you.

'East Birmingham has a higher proportion of pre-school children than the national average (7.9% compared with 6.5%)' – WMRHA 1988 Final Home Population Estimates.

'East Birmingham inner city wards form a band of deprivatrion which is ranked in the worst 2.5% in the country. 90% of electoral districts in the UK are less deprived than the inner city parts of East Birmingham' – Department of Environment Z score (based on social class, ethnicity, unemployment, overcrowding, lack of basic amenities, single parents and pensioners living alone).

'The scores for East Birmingham indicate greater deprivation than the City average' – Townsend Index of Deprivation (based on four census variables: unemployment; car ownership; overcrowding; not being an owner/occupier).

'Unemployment is very unevenly distributed across the City with inner city Parliamentary constituencies experiencing both the highest absolute numbers, and highest rates of unemployment' – Labour Market Information Bulletin 1991 published by Economic Development Division.

'74% of the Asian mothers had received no formal education and 71% were illiterate in their own language. 83% of the Asian mothers were not fluent in English and 90% stated they required an interpreter to communicate fully with English speakers' – East Birmingham Health Authority Antenatal Care Research Project: First Year Report. Dance, J. and Hughes, C., 1987.

I find the facts and figures alarming even though I have lived and worked in East Birmingham for most of my life. What they prove is what you feel: That this area needs us badly and that our inner city strategy is right.

Tony Henry.

Tony Henry reinforced the synonymity, for him, between quality and equality by accompanying the letter with an article he had written in which he uses emotive 'visionary' terms to describe what quality means for him:

> The point I am trying to make is that quality in an organisation is either there or it isn't. You cannot bring it into an organisation through BS 5750 or TQM. What those systems can do is to protect quality and if quality is in the organisation it will be identified by whatever quality assurance systems are devised.
>
> Quality is about customer delight rather than customer satisfaction. It is about total staff involvement rather than hierarchical top-down system imposition. It is about incremental quality improvement rather than giant leaps. It is about living, loving, passion, fighting, cherishing, nurturing, struggling, crying, laughing...' (Henry, 1991, p.15)

In order to further aid customer responsiveness and to accommodate the burgeoning inner-city network, the organization of the College has undergone a series of transformations. The trend has been towards a 'flatter' less hierarchical structure, summed up in the aphorism 'simple form, lean staff' (heralding the section on organizational structure in the 1989–90 development plan).

The consequence of the 'flattening' process is that the number of senior managers has been reduced, with responsibility and budgets devolved to curriculum programme areas. Currently there are 16 such areas, each led by a programme area leader. Cross-college functions such as learning development, opportunities development, student development and organizational development are the responsibility of programme leaders. Quality development and support rests with four quality improvement leaders (see Figure 12.1).

The difficulty with the heady mix of change as the norm, the 'vision' thing, the atomistic customer and loving and trusting everybody and deferring decisions to the 'front-line' is that order and control can quickly disappear. It was a recognition of this that led to the decision being taken in 1990 to begin a move towards installing a quality control system capable of achieving BS 5750 certification. The intention was that the system would inject procedural controls

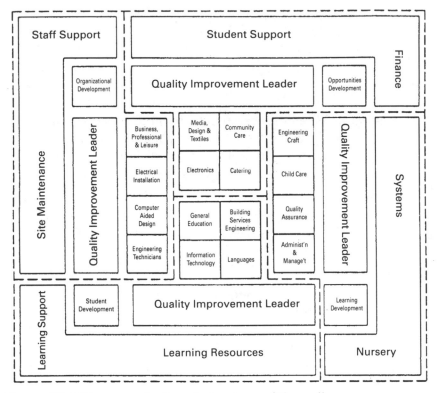

Figure 12.1 The organizational structure of the college

and documentation capable of introducing stability and sustaining quality. A further factor influencing the adoption of the policy was the pressing need to respond to the College's industrial customers.

Whatever the traumas of economic decline locally, the College has retained strong links with surviving industry. As companies have been forced to introduce or reaffirm quality control mechanisms, suppliers, including the College, have been expected to follow the lead or risk losing the business.

The System

Introducing BS 5750, designed as it is for manufacturing, into a service organization creates the problem of deciding what the organization's 'product' should be. Some colleges have designated the student as the 'product' and have designed quality assurance systems to match. For East Birmingham College it was decided that its 'product' should be the course of study, with the quality assurance system designed to support delivery. A focal point of the system is the course team handbook. Accessible to everyone, the handbook contains procedures and records of the weekly course team meetings. Meetings are supported by the provision of one hour's remission from teaching for every member of staff to attend on Friday mornings; as a result the College is closed to customers between 9 and 10 a.m. One intention of the gathering is to act as a 'quality circle' in terms of curriculum form and delivery; accordingly, both customers and support staff are included in the team's make up.

The course team handbook also underpins the internal auditor programme during the course of which trained staff, from unconnected curriculum areas, monitor procedural compliance. Lack of compliance, or non-conformance, leads to the issuing of a notice and the requirement that things are corrected within a set period, the process being monitored by the quality manager. The introduction of tight quality control and industry-derived methods has resulted in better monitoring of performance indicators. Such monitoring has extended to include the impact of equal opportunity policies and measuring the extent of support by individual curriculum areas for the College's inner-city strategy. This backing, from a seemingly unlikely source, has proved a powerful means of assisting policy implementation.

Conclusion

The achievement of BS 5750 has enabled the College to retain and strengthen its industrial customer base. All the same, there is a feeling amongst those East Birmingham College staff involved in assisting industry in the introduction of quality procedures and techniques that the College's system tends to be over-complex and in need of simplification. A further problem is the belief, amongst some staff, that once British Standard certification had been accomplished then quality was finished with. Mortiboys and Oakland (1991) have noted, in a series of case studies, that this is not uncommon and that the achievement of BS 5750 can lead to complacency and the belief that quality has been achieved once and for all by reaching certain minimum standards. Price (1990) has also pointed out that such over-reliance on the system is counter-productive:

> A system is essential. But a system is only a system nothing more. A
> system cannot build quality into a product any more than scaffolding can

build a pile of bricks into a house. It is a framework, within which work is done. It is all structure, all form, and no content (p.78).

The intention by senior managers to add content, by using the system to underpin a controlled return to the College's former expansive quality movement, has been hindered by the College's move to incorporation. This has both distracted attention and re-emphasized the need for strict organizational and financial control. Inevitably, with jobs and survival on the line, there is caution and constraint about backing every customer-inspired innovation in the hope that, perhaps, some might be successful.

A further factor influencing the current shape and direction of quality has been the continuing recession. This has led to a refocusing of the College's inner-city mission. The result has been that successful customized training programmes, linked to jobs with local companies, have been replaced by franchised University of Central England courses. The partnership, modelled on the American Community College system, is intended to ensure that local degrees go to local people. The effect of this emergent relationship has been that some realignment has been necessary in order to interface with the University's quality system. Notwithstanding this new partnership, the quality infrastructure exists to reawaken, when required, former associations.

When Venables conducted her 1967 case study into FE's role, focused as it was on East Birmingham College, she was able to report that the student population of the College was made up of young white males on day-release from local engineering companies, supported by white male teachers recruited from the same source. The intervening years of economic and social change have transformed the College's curriculum and clientele to the extent that female students now form just under 50 per cent of the student population, with ethnic minority students accounting for 35 per cent of all students. There has also been a sharp and continued rise in the number of adults using the College. The reshaping of the College's market has been matched by a change to the personnel in the College with large increases in the numbers of women and ethnic minority staff. Additionally, many of the management roles within the College are now filled by women, including the three vice-principal posts.

East Birmingham College has been at the forefront of FE's acknowledgement of the importance of quality to institutional survival and growth. However, the College has extended this to add a moral dimension by linking quality with equality of opportunity for its local community. Furthermore, in responding to its long-standing links with industry, the College has managed to blend together its former and current mission.

With its well-established quality system capable, when events allow, of continuing the journey into TQM, East Birmingham College appears to be set fair. Nevertheless, a cause for concern, for some, is Blyton and Turnbull's (1992) identification of the contradictions within the humanistic elements of TQM which they believe leads to greater worker subordination. By contrast, the distinctive version of quality abroad at East Birmingham College is founded on looking outwards to the community as a way of shaping relationships and philosophies internally and is, arguably, more to do with addressing inequality than inefficiency and is more about laughing and loving than crying.

Chapter 13
Operating beyond BS 5750 in a Training Centre

Keith Sanders

Introduction

I am proud to say that I now own a computer that has only just become obsolete. One almost envies those who lived in the twelfth and thirteenth centuries when change was hardly discernible from one generation to another. Now we find, just as we at Kent Training Centres thought we had done well to be amongst the very first training establishments to get the much-lauded BS 5750, that it is in danger of being eclipsed by the latest initiative, Investors in People. I feel almost apologetic about talking about something so old-fashioned as BS 5750. Is the apparent decline in the popularity of BS 5750 another indication of the rapidity with which changes take place? As this is being written, we are forewarned of impending changes to the requirements of BS 5750.

A Major Commitment of Resources

Whatever way you look at it, a great deal of time and energy has to be committed to getting 'quality' accreditation. I'm not sure what's worse: having a small number of staff with one or two people spending an alarming amount of their time beavering away to get the BS 5750 or trying to marshal a mass of people, each doing their little bit. Either way the volume, not to say frenzy, of activity can finish up making the attainment of the accolade an end in itself. This is quite understandable. Any initial attempt to comprehend the inscrutable texts that accompany the official BS 5750 standard documentation is daunting enough. Seeking to mould some sort of response to the jargon that fits one's own organization looks all but impossible.

For the attainment of Part 1 there are 20 sections to be addressed, one less for Part 2 (the details of the sections are set out in Chapter 1). Even a cursory glance at these sections will reveal a few that do not immediately suggest how they might apply to an enlightened educational environment e.g., '4.13 Control of non-conforming product'. The more thoroughly the document, 'Quality Systems. Part 1. Specification for design/development, production, installation and servicing' is reviewed, the greater the task of interpretation appears.

Selecting the Right Target

There is a reward for all this industry, of course. We are prepared to make the huge effort required safe in the knowledge that once we have completed the documentation and been certificated then we can relax and take time to bask in the glory of a job well done. In the process, we've made it clear what we aspire to do, even what we could do if everyone allowed us to get on with our work without constant interference.

Seeking not to judge others by my own standards, I'm prepared to bet that practically everyone who has been involved in the massive task of getting any quality standard paperwork to its final stage will have lost sight of what it's all about on several occasions. The essential truth is that, during this period of frenetic activity, it is important to bear in mind that attaining quality certification is not an end in itself. To do so will undoubtedly make for a very rough road when the time comes to try and live with the ideals set down on the certificated Tablets of Stone. There is life after the certificate arrives.

In the early stages, it is all too easy to lose sight of the fact that the purpose of the attainment of BS 5750, Investors in People, TQM, TQE, ISO 9000, etc., is to improve, measurably, the operation of your enterprise. Human beings are startlingly adept at kidding themselves into believing all sorts of half-truths. It may even be that you think the whole business of BS 5750 and the like is a big propaganda confidence trick. It is possible that this is the case. Presuming, however, that you've been seduced into going for it, there's no long-term value in setting all sorts of laudable, but ultimately unattainable targets.

We've all been told to take more exercise. But it's only if that exercise comes as a natural part of our daily activity, or at least can be moulded to become so, that there is really any chance of keeping it up for any length of time. It's just the same with quality. If it doesn't fairly reflect the sort of activity that goes on anyway, it is going to become no more than an aggravating mass of paperwork that has little or no relevance to day-to-day activity.

Traps for the Unwary

In seeking to attain any quality standard, the target must be as close as possible to what you were aiming at anyway. There are those who felt that going for BS 5750 was an opportunity to clean up their act. Don't try it. Attempting to effect too much change through and during the implementation of BS 5750 or any other quality system will promote a majestic list of disasters. Some of the more obvious ones are:

- When the time comes for assessment it will be very difficult to be able to bring forward evidence in ample quantity to satisfy BSI or other assessors if you have included a mass of information on new ideals that have yet to be tried and tested. It is, however, comparatively easy if all you have to do is show what you are already doing, albeit a bit tidied up. You will gain certification only by being able to demonstrate the operation of your quality system. The production of a magnificent, but largely peripheral, document, will not gain your certification.
- If you have decided to introduce a whole swath of new ambitions, you must accept that you have let yourself in for an enormous amount of work in the actual production of new forms and new systems. You will have to spend a great deal of time briefing all relevant personnel. The new procedures must be monitored and amended where necessary. Attaining the certification depends on an ability to demonstrate how well the organization is adhering to your quality systems. This is more difficult when half the systems are unfamiliar to the organization.
- If a high proportion of the system is new, it is highly likely that a significant proportion will prove at best in need of major modification, at worst entirely unsustainable. Such a situation will provide valuable evidence for those concerned to pour scorn on the whole idea of trying to devise and implement the quality system.
- An increasing proportion of the working population are or perceive themselves to be working under stressful circumstances. The imposition of a mountain of unfamiliar extra chores aggravates this situation. There is a risk of alienating the very people upon whom the success of the implementation of BS 5750

depends.
- The risk of a nervous breakdown.

What is Quality Anyway?

To digress. Apart from the greengrocers which advertised 'Quality Tomatoes', it seems to me that quality was not a word that stood on its own in my formative years. You had good quality, inferior quality, high quality. When did its solo use start? Even worse what does 'total quality' mean? There is a carelessness about the use of 'quality' that does not auger well for those involved in seeking to attain some kind of assessment of managerial accomplishment and activity. A clear idea of what you mean by quality as it applies to your day-to-day activity is essential. It might well be that aspiring to a 'slightly better quality' is a worthwhile and attainable ambition.

Kent Training Centres

At Kent Training Centres in Dover, we made a decision that we would go for BS 5750. My wife's employers were going through an apparently nebulous activity called TQM. This sounded all very well but appeared to be like starting a building with the construction of the third floor. BS 5750 seemed to provide an ideal framework and discipline upon which to construct other improvements to management.

The briefest of descriptions of what Kent Training Centres (KTC) do: we were set up in 1988 to provide training for the construction industry. The construction of the channel tunnel was in full swing and there were other important associated civil engineering projects. Many towns in East Kent were poised to enter a new phase of expansion and housing development. It was clearly essential that this burgeoning construction industry had its training needs met adequately. All sorts of august bodies sought and supported our establishment.

The construction industry went on to become one of the severest casualties of the recession which started in 1990 and showed few signs of improvement four years later. Kent Training Centre's existence has coincided with a heady peak of construction activity followed by a very deep trough. The experience has demonstrated that flexibility is amongst the greatest of virtues. Perhaps we made a virtue of necessity? There was no hope of survival if we failed to respond appropriately to ever-changing circumstances.

We had already set about addressing the cost-effectiveness of our training. A wide variety of short and long courses were operated. In our early days, construction skills were identified as being in short supply. Government training schemes (in 1988 the newly devised Employment Training) placed emphasis on development of high quality training for unemployed adults. Initial six-month City and Guilds courses were offered. Later KTC went on to pioneer the provision of training and assessment for the construction industry's NVQs in Kent. With an encouragingly high standard of qualifications gained by trainees, combined with the attainment of a steady decrease in the hourly costs of training, we continued to fulfil cost-effectiveness criteria whilst maintaining a high quality of training.

We cooperated with the Construction Industry Training Board and a number of local and national employers in organizing well-received tailor-made short courses in a wide array of construction craft skills. It seemed logical for a new company, already wedded to innovation, to actively consider BS 5750. We were accustomed to the careful scrutiny of what we did and how we did it.

The Commitment

BS 5750 was still a relatively new concept when we made the decision to seek its attainment. The BSI document 'Guidance Notes for the Application of ISO 9000/EN 29000/BS 5750' had yet to be published. Such 'explanations' as then existed were clearly aimed at manufacturing industry. We decided to seek the advice of a consultant. The consultant's background was industrial. The BS 5750 stemmed, we were told, in no small measure from the stringent quality control systems imposed on their suppliers by the Ministry of Defence.

The role that the consultant played in producing a final draft was considerable. He readily admitted, however, that it was hard to apply some standards to our type of operation. As we had done with NVQs, we found ourselves sailing in uncharted waters.

In defining responses to the demands of the standards, we felt ourselves hampered by a combination of ambiguity and inscrutable text. For example, in considering the definitions of Section 4.7 'Purchaser supplied product', we were exercised for some time in deciding whether the training courses were the 'product', or the trainees. There were some categories which we eventually decided just did not apply, e.g., 4.20 'Statistical Techniques'.

We did have one major bit of luck. Our consultant advised us that the quality manual itself would be hard and expensive to alter once it had been accepted by BSI, so we tried to make sure that the manual provided as much scope as possible for later variation. This was good advice for, even though we have subsequently found out that the manual is not quite as difficult to revise as we were initially led to believe, it immediately made us think about building in flexibility in the production and application of the manual.

The development process involved the production of a broad response to each section of the standard. Decisions were then made as to how to share the response between what would be included in the quality manual itself and what would be laid out in the operational procedures. Clearly each section of the 'standard' would require a corresponding response in the manual. In turn each section of the manual would be supported by one or more operational procedures. The procedures themselves would often relate to the use of annotated forms, some domestic, others produced by outside organizations. We prepared the required 20 sections in the quality manual; we generated far more operational procedures. It was also vital to continually cross-reference responses to avoid both duplication and omission.

We sought to ensure that the manual would not proscribe subsequent change. It could not, however, be so bland as to be so much pap. We crossed the i's and dotted the t's in the production of the associated quality procedures and proformas which we could, within reason, alter as often as circumstances required. Early progress seemed very slow; nevertheless as we progressed, we became ever more gratified that, after each meeting with the consultant, the inclusion of our suggested revisions, expansions, redefinitions, etc., did seem to be getting us measurably closer to a complete manual. During the development of the the manual itself, I had taken on the job of writing all the quality procedures and standardizing the forms we used.

A Pitfall

Pride, they say, cometh before a fall. Something which I had briefly worried about now occurred to our consultant. Were we *designing* anything? Well, yes. We designed training courses, we designed training manuals, we designed workshop facilities; it was a pretty extensive list. Those of you with the wisdom of hindsight will be astonished at our lack of perspicacity. We had been going for BS 5750 Part 2, when really we ought to be going for Part 1. Looking back, this didn't finish up making nearly as big an impact on our progress as we then feared. It certainly looked pretty daunting at the time. It now became necessary to address the requirements of Part 1, Section 4.4, 'Design control'. In hindsight I have paused to consider that what we did was, in effect, to bolt a response to this section onto an existing framework. It might be that this is the reason why the implementation of this section has caused us the most serious problems.

It was at about the same time that the draft guidelines were produced by BSI for those seeking to apply BS 5750 to education and training. They were of some assistance in tidying up a few misunderstandings, but a good deal of ambiguity remained. Possibly because we weren't a mainstream educational institution (if such a thing exists), some issues became even more obscured.

A Usable Guide or a Straitjacket?

I've already mentioned that I set about writing our operational procedures. If the emerging documents were to have any real value, they would have to provide a source of information and guidance for both existing and new staff. Our resolve to produce something practical and workable made it necessary first to write down what we were actually doing, where this had not already been done. Many of the things we were doing must have been pretty good otherwise we wouldn't have been getting the results we were. There were cases where it was necessary to negotiate a common approach where differences existed between one discipline and another.

Some of the operational procedures, when written out, became very convoluted indeed. On such occasions it seemed more appropriate to attempt a flow chart. An example was how we set about administering the employment training scheme to meet the requirements of the Job Centres, Benefits Agency and Kent TEC. Figure 13.1 shows that flow chart as later amended to cope with the new Training for Work Scheme. Producing the hundreds of pages of procedures, designing some new forms, annotating and revising existing forms, would have been pretty impractical for me without the aid of a computer. Where flow charts were not appropriate, text was put together by word-processing. Many of the initial efforts were Aunt Sallys. Only an ability to make modifications with ease made the task approachable. There are those within any organization who, without an ability to operate computers themselves, enthusiastically grasp the fact that changes can be made without too much of a

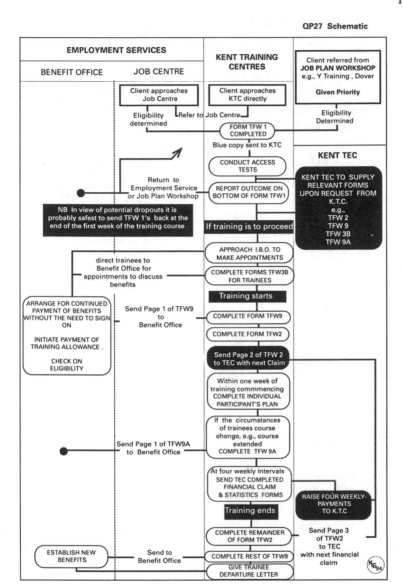

Figure 13.1 Administering the Employment Training scheme

problem. The umpteenth request for change can make one wish for the return of parchment and quill.

The value of setting everything down on a computer to facilitate our initial amendments was considerable. It has been even more useful, however, to be able to modify and revise in the light of snags that have emerged as we operated the systems. This has been especially true when small modifications have been desirable. If it hadn't been possible to effect these small changes with such relative ease I am sure we would have rationalized leaving things as they were.

Each standard text operational procedure tried to maintain a uniform layout containing three basic sections. The first gave a background to the matters covered and the circumstances under which we worked. New members of staff would first need to be introduced to what we were doing and what resources were available before telling them how we went about the associated tasks in the second section. This prescribed how the work was to be carried out. To cut down on the number of operational procedures an effort was made to address as many differing circumstances as possible. The third part listed the various areas of activity and those with responsibility for their implementation. Figure 13.2, an initial attempt, since much revised, indicates the basic layout.

Internal Audits

Early on in the development of our quality systems, an important issue emerged. We have a relatively small staff establishment. We certainly do not have the luxury of a quality control section, but we did have to consider the question of internal auditing in addressing Section 4.17 of the Part 1 Standard (4.16 for Part 2). It became clear that we would have to try, wherever feasible, to leave our managing director in a position in which he would be able to carry out audits. This we did by omitting him from immediate day-to-day involvement in the application of the quality system, otherwise he would be forever auditing himself, clearly an unacceptable state of affairs. The question of who is going to carry out internal auditing needs to be considered at an early stage; this is especially so for a company with a small number of employees. Many smaller schools must face just such a situation, where there may be only three or four 'levels'. This problem is, even now, being further aggregated by the move to 'flatten' management structures yet further as part of a commitment to Investors in People. Bear in mind that there are senior staff who remain uncomfortable about being audited by their juniors.

In our case it was decided that the centre manager would be the management representative (see 4.1.2.3. in the 'Standard'):

> The supplier shall appoint a management representative who, irrespective of other responsibilities, shall have defined authority and responsibility for ensuring that the requirements of this International Standard are implemented and maintained.

KENT TRAINING CENTRES LTD.,
QUALITY MANUAL

OPERATING PROCEDURES & PRO-FORMAE

QP3 TELEPHONE ENQUIRIES.

Background

The External Telephone System enables calls to be connected to the Administrative Office and the office of the Managing Director. Calls once received can be transferred to and from any phone.

There is also an internal telephone system connected to the various work areas, but not connected in any way to external lines.

Procedures

a. All incoming telephone calls will be recorded in the telephone book. It is the responsibility of the person who receives the call to make the entry. The book will be maintained in the Administrative Office.

b. Where the call cannot be dealt with satisfactorily by the initial receiver of the call, the call will be transferred to the appropriate KTC employee .

c. Where this is not possible a message will be taken to include the following information:

- ☎ The date and time of the call
- ☎ The name of the caller.
- ☎ Where appropriate, the name of the company employing the caller
- ☎ The telephone number where the caller can be reached.
- ☎ Any message the caller wishes to be relayed to include wherever possible the purpose of the call.

d. This message will be taken on the form provided, the top copy relayed to the appropriate person and a copy retained by the person taking the initial call.

e. The recipient of the message will sign the copy held by the original receiver of the call once the appropriate action has been undertaken.

RESPONSIBILITY

To answer a call   Any KTC employee in the vicinity
To record call in phone book   Receiver of the Call
Relaying Message   Receiver of the Call
Signing copy of message form   Designated message recipient.

Approved .... Issue No. 1   Date December 10 1991

Figure 13.2 Example of operating procedures: telephone enquiries

Despite all our care, there were instanceswhere we could not maintain the managing director's independence. For a small minority of the internal audits we engaged the services of an 'outsider'.

It is, of course, necessary to show the assessor that your auditor is suitably qualified. Appropriate one-day quality audit courses are widely available. Our managing director undertook such a course.

The very process of concentrating on how the quality system would be applied and administered reinforced the need to ensure we avoided blind canyons. There could be no value in creating paperwork that proscribed change. It is one of BS 5750's most serious flaws that, if ill-applied, it can smother change. We sought to ensure, from the very start, that our quality system reflected what we could reasonably expect to do, indeed, as far as possible, what we were already doing. At the same time we recognized that our activities would change.

Detecting change or realizing where we have strayed from the stated quality systems is not always an easy process. Internal audits highlight 'non-compliances'. These are occasions, of varying degrees of gravity, where the standard, as described, has not been attained. Quite often this occurs where small, often imperceptible, changes in our activities have taken place in response to new situations or demands. The ongoing assessments made by the British Standards Institute have also thrown up similar non-compliances. These may result from the fact that our operations have made it difficult to bring forward appropriate or sufficient evidence to show that we are actually doing what we said we were going to do. Non-compliances are usually resolved by either reverting to the original straight-and-narrow where we have strayed, or revising procedures to reflect changing situations.

Situations have most certainly changed on several fronts. Whilst BS 5750 has been in place at Kent Training Centres, Construction Industry Training Board support for government training for adults ended; Training for Work has replaced Employment Training; an array of new health and safety requirements has emerged and refuses to be ignored. All these have required amendments to our operational procedures.

The construction industry is in disarray. Building companies rely more and more on sub-contracting work to an ever-increasing number of ever-smaller building enterprises. The huge majority of construction companies have, as a primary and often sole objective, survival. Training comes very low on the list of priorities. There has been a qualitative and quantitative change in the range of commercial training sought and offered. We have become increasingly involved with and committed to training for those concerned with the conservation of our built heritage.

Finding the Time

The operation, auditing and revision of the quality system has, of course, to be fitted in to all our other day-to-day activities. A need to amend a form that hasn't worked, or a procedure that no longer fits the circumstances isn't always a welcome chore. There have been several occasions when internal audits have caused surprise that we have innocently strayed so far from our original intended path. There have, however, been no changes that have been so daunting as to militate against change and improvement. This must surely be because we expected and legislated for change.

Counting the Cost

Have the significant costs and commitment of time to attaining and maintaining BS 5750 been worthwhile? I feel they undoubtedly have. The mind has been concentrated. It has given our operations yardsticks against which to measure corporate and individual performance. I'm not sure whether it has been quite the promised prestigious commercial advantage, but we have certainly gained kudos and prestige from attaining the award. The very existence and implementation of a quality system has enhanced our corporate performance. The book of operating procedures does prove a useful reference. We are more generally more careful.

It has to be admitted that we have paused to wonder at the charges imposed upon us by BSI for initial certification and their ongoing assessments. We hear that there are those who have got to the point where they could apply for and, they tell us, obtain certification, but have held back because of the cost. I paused for some time before deciding to leave readers to make their own assessment of such a strategy.

Many Go out for Wool and Come Home Shorn

Someone who didn't think, as they set about documenting their quality standards, of a rapidly changing life after attaining certification would now have a different story to tell. They would have found themselves toiling under an ill-fitting yoke. They will be finding it hard to respond to change without major disruption to their quality system. They will, by now, probably have decided that the whole thing was a waste of time and money. And that will be a shame for there is nothing so irksome as expending time, energy and money in producing a gilded top quality stick with which to beat yourself.

Chapter 14

Right Second Time: TQM in the In-service Training of Professionals

Phil Stephenson

Introduction

I have found inspiration in the messages of Total Quality Management but was keen to see how much of the quality message I could transfer from theory to practice to help enhance one aspect of my current work: the preparation, delivery and follow-up of in-service training events. The first real opportunity to present itself was a training afternoon for 43 people – 26 support staff, 14 teachers and three headteachers – on the subject of developing a working partnership between ancillary support staff and teachers. The group represented mainstream primary schools in the Hastings area. This chapter describes what happened and offers a positive step forward based on my experience of putting TQM theory into practice: a set of criteria against which in-service training could be planned or measured – The Ten Training Triggers.

Context

I work as part of a team of four advisory teachers with close links with the educational psychologists. One recent area of need raised by our schools was how best to use ancillary support in the class-room, predominantly but not exclusively for those children with special educational needs. Schools were using more ancillary staff but were not always sure of how best to use them. I decided this provided me with a great opportunity to put my TQM theory into practice. Unlike Crosby (1979) I did not feel I would get it 'right first time' but perhaps 'right second time'.

Quality Challenges

Many of the TQM gurus seem obsessed with measuring quality and expressing their main messages as numbered statements with punchy titles (Deming's 14 points for management, Juran's ten steps for quality improvement, Crosby's 14 steps). A few years ago I would have measured the quality of in-service training events by using the four Ms:

Meals	was it a good lunch?
Motivation	was the speaker inspiring?
Mixing	was there a chance to meet and mingle?
Means	was there a means by which I could use this training back in the busy classroom?

Invariably courses would score one to three Ms, but rarely four. I believe the quality of training should be measured and its usefulness evaluated but feel a more sophisticated measuring device should supersede the four Ms. Here I present the Ten Training Triggers and then describe the process which led to their formulation. I have found them useful when planning and evaluating my own training and offer them as a starting point on the journey to quality.

The Ten Training Triggers

T1. Training should be action based – the training should be easy to translate into action for every participant using the tools and techniques of TQM .

T2. Training should be capable of translation – what should each participant (and school) do before they return to school to help back at school?

T3. There should be some motivation to use the training message - an active means of supporting the course participants and giving them a source for feedback.

T4. Training should involve sharing – opportunities to share viewpoints and establish where individuals are in terms of the training message and to explore where they want to go.

T5. Training should have local elements and provide a strong case for change – being able to link in local practice is very important and should be used constructively to supplement general (national) research in order to clarify the need or opportunity for change.

T6. Provide a mechanism to facilitate change – provide a means by which individuals or teams can take the first few steps in translating the training message into practice at school. This fits in with Peters' (1989) theory that if training messages are not acted upon within 72 hours their impact is negligible.

T7. Provide a non-threatening framework – the course member should leave the training session with a better than even chance of effecting change once back in their own establishment.

T8. If possible involve all concerned parties – involve as many people as possible, but certainly representatives of those in the 'front line' or in a position to strongly influence the changes necessary.

T9. Offer support and follow up to the schools – a measure of support available from the trainer to help support developments in school (i.e., after the course).

T10. Provide training at a time when participants are fresh – although this runs into difficulties with cost, the advantages may well outweigh the disadvantages.

Underpinning the quality challenges as I see them are five basic principles.

1. Quality is everyone's business. The need for everyone to become involved in the process of quality improvement is crucial. Every person, every process, every interaction has to reflect upon the total quality of what is being attempted. This was particularly pertinent to my training session as many of the participants had recognized the need for everyone to be involved or compliant but did not know what to do next.

2. Quality is what the customer says it is (Feigenbaum, 1983). I found an interesting parallel with the NHS and their evaluation of TQM. Kogan *et al.* (1991) found that most senior managers decided for themselves what the customers (in school terms, staff, parents and pupils) wanted or needed. It was only when things began to go wrong that the customers' needs and perceptions were sought. This ties in with my original feeling that in education we are more likely to get it right second (or third) time rather than Crosby's first time. TQM is a process not an end product, so the notion of continual improvement is tied in to clear outcomes, acuity to customers' needs and the flexibility to change and redirect.

3. The rules of the game according to Deming (1982). The key to better management lies in the study of the processes by which we get things done in order to analyse quality failure. This seemed a good starting point to me. He differentiates between special and common causes of failure. Common causes are related to a systems failure so that changes need to be made to the process or procedure. Special causes relate to procedures or rules that are not followed; individual changes need to be made to ensure compliance. Relating this to the group, it was interesting to note the common causes of failure rated highly in that most schools acknowledged the absence of any system, policy or agreement. As West-Burnham (1992) points out, if values are not explicit they are not capable of implementation. A failure to articulate requirements makes conformity difficult and so the process and quality break down.

The main initial area of concern for both teaching and ancillary staff was the fact that some teachers did not use support staff as well as others and were lackadaisical about their ability to alter this. The main challenge seemed to hinge on the absence of any agreed system. Without an agreement or procedures on how best to use support staff there could be no special causes of failure, as the procedures or rules were not established in the first place. There seemed to be recognition both from research and school-based knowledge that there is a right way to form a working partnership between teachers and ancillaries; my aim was to provide a forum and a vehicle to allow us to get it right second time.

Crosby (1979) argues for a culture change away from expecting errors to a philosophy of zero defects. Comments during the session like: 'We know that when we go in Mrs T's room we will not be well used' or, 'We can't get Mr H to cooperate with us' or, 'It is working really well in the infants but not with the juniors', all add weight to the argument that not only do there need to be agreed rules but also a team approach to achieve quality. In order to effectively move forward quality must be measured across the entire school, not in isolation.

4. A team approach? Another major area of concern was the lack of a team approach. For two of the schools represented, the training session was the first time the support staff and teacher had actually been able to meet and discuss these issues! TQM offers a team approach to problem solving through the use of quality circles or quality teams. Many of the tools and techniques, although not traditionally used, are relatively easily applied in an educational setting. Many schools found there was an absence of time to meet, let alone opportunities to problem solve or talk quality. I hoped that the style of my delivery, as much as the message itself, might help with this difficulty back in schools.

A lot of TQM literature focuses on the need for a quality team culture. Murgatroyd and Morgan (1992) talk of the three Cs of

TQM:

Culture	– values that bind an organization
Commitment	– shared goals and values
Communication	– awareness, openness, feedback.

All of these were crucial issues mentioned by both teaching and ancillary staff and yet progress towards them had been very difficult. I wanted to join with Juran (1988) and make my recipe for action 90 per cent substance and 10 per cent exhortation.

5. *Where's the boss? Who's the boss?* Juran (1988) insists that quality improvement begins at the top level of management. His comments have irritated senior managers and probably would have the same effect on headteachers. One major challenge I was very aware of before the course was how I could help to empower those attending the course to effect change back in their schools.

The Quality Improvement Project – The Training Session

Pre-course publicity – I made it very clear that the session would be for representatives from both the teaching and ancillary staff (T8), that the session would review local and national research (T5) and a framework for development would be offered (T1, T6, T7). Another plus factor was that different schools were represented, so a less insular view was possible (T4).

The session itself – I decided to hold the session on a Friday afternoon during school time (T10). This was an attempt to avoid disruption but actually meant that some of the ancillaries (mostly employed part-time) came in their own time, which was not my intention (and contravened T10!). I welcomed the group, explained my aims and tried to put everyone at ease.

Establishing a baseline – the first activity was designed to establish baselines of where the ancillaries felt they were at the moment and to record the areas of strength and difficulty. This provided a gentle introduction and gave the group some reassurance (see Table 14.1). I also found it useful to have some statistics. I was quite surprised to see that the course members were particularly interested in the quantitative data.

Statement	Very True	Partly True	Untrue
1. I enjoy what I do	91	9	0
2. I am anxious about my ability to do the job	4	38	58
3. I am kept well informed about what is happening in the school	38	58	4
4. I am kept well informed about the children I work with	38	56	6
5. I am valued by the school	85	15	0
6. I am clear what I can and cannot do in my job	56	42	2

(n=38)

Table 14.1 Ancillary responses (in percentages)

Establishing Benchmarks – to achieve this I asked the group to separate into ancillaries and teachers. The ancillaries answered the questions shown in Tables 14.2 and 14.3 (the number in brackets after each statement relates to the number of times the statement was made.)

To have time set aside to discuss issues with teachers (9)
To have more variety of jobs in classroom (4)
To have (more) time to prepare (4)
To take more on and not be underestimated (3)
To have more support from staff (3)
For time not to be spread too thinly (2)
More money !! (2)
To have a higher profile (1)

Table 14.2 Ancillary responses to: 'What would help to make your job even more enjoyable?'

To know in advance what I have to do (9)
To have more time (8)
Better communications (6)
More information from class teacher (5)
More training (5)
Not to be spread too thinly (3)
More variety of duties (3)
Opportunities for qualifications (2)
Time to prepare (2)

Table 14.3 Ancillary responses to: 'What would help you to do your job more effectively?'

I asked the teachers to address the questions shown in Tables 14.4 and 14.5.

More involvement (8)
More variety (4)
Provide opportunities for feedback (2)
Explain reasons for doing things (2)
Listen to the ancillary and their needs (2)
Develop into a teamwork and partnership (1)

Table 14.4 Teachers' responses to: 'What do you feel would help to make the ancillary's job even more enjoyable'

Joint planning with the teacher (10)
In-house and external training (8)
Regular time to talk (8)
Opportunity to share problems (4)
Guidelines for job description (2)
To receive thanks (1)
Equal status in the pupils' eyes (1)

Table 14.5 Teachers' responses to: 'What do you feel would help to make the ancillary's job even more effective?'

We found that there was a high level of agreement between the two groups and shared this with everyone. This reinforced the next stage which was for me to present the local and national research to provide a theoretical basis for change (T5). There was broad agreement that the views of the assembled group and the findings presented were closely matched, which provided a strong foundation upon which to build. The inevitable next step was to look at reasons for quality failure and link them to Deming's common and special causes for failure. Among cries of 'We know some teachers don't use ancillaries properly but what can we do?', we established the need for action (T1).

Critical success factors – the next step was to decide upon the critical success factors for a quality working relationship between ancillary and the school. This was easy, as agreement had already been reached on factors affecting both effectiveness and enjoyment (Tables 14.1 – 14.5, plus research findings). The key issue seemed to be achieving conformity towards a quality working relationship between ancillary and teacher within the school. We decided that a vehicle or mechanism for establishing good practice would be needed to convert these critical success factors into positive benchmarks.

The least threatening way of doing this (T7) was for us to produce a fictional booklet/policy on the effective use of ancillaries which drew together all the issues we had raised and provided a positive framework for development. This would be a booklet where ideal practice would be recorded in a way that participating schools could use it as a basis for developing quality. We worked in mixed groups so that both teachers and ancillaries were represented, in effect forming quality circles, although many were not aware of this at the time! Using headings, each group recorded what they felt should be included in the booklet. Two days later a 15-page booklet was put together and hastily circulated to the participating schools to maintain the momentum of the training initiative (T3). I tried to make the booklet look quite professional but not too heavy so that if it were circulated within the school it would generate some interest.

The booklet is now being used in schools as a sourcebook of good or ideal practice as determined by a group of practicing professionals, and I think it has been respected because of everyone's close involvement in the process. I have received quite a number of requests for the booklet but have decided that the best way of facilitating this enthusiasm from other schools is to repeat the training next term. Schools not directly involved in the process may find the booklet more difficult to use.

Before the course participants left the session I asked for a volunteer from each school to be responsible for reporting back to me on the progress they had made and the challenges they had faced when they got back to school. The letter was dated two weeks after the training session and became known as the 'Dear Phil' letter! (T3). This proved very effective in spurring them on to action (T1) and seemed to motivate people both in the short and long term. I received a 100 per cent response and many of the returns were very detailed. On the forms and at the end of the session I offered my services to help and support at school level (T9). This option, so far, has been taken up by 60 per cent of the schools represented.

Evaluation of the Product – The Success of the Training Approach; a Question of Impact

It was interesting to receive feedback from all the schools and in a qualitative way measure the impact on school's practice. The following were mentioned as significant changes by the schools in the feedback letters or my visit to the school:

- Meetings were established between ancillaries and teachers, and ancillaries also met as a group. Representatives were chosen to meet with staff or the headteacher. Meetings became more regular and formalized. (e.g., minutes taken, etc.).
- A whole-staff discussion was established using the course booklet as a catalyst; the current working system was critically reviewed by those operating it (i.e. the whole school!). The need for change was recognized and alternative ways of working were developed.
- The need for a school document on effective use of the ancillary was established to address the need for conformity.
- Current needs were recognized; in some cases further, more personalized INSET was requested. The need for an annual appraisal review for ancillaries was built in.
- The need for meetings between teaching and ancillary staff was established to allow effective forward planning.
- The need for induction of new ancillaries so that the work done to establish effective working practice was perpetuated.

The feedback I received, both through the 'Dear Phil' letters and personal visits was extremely encouraging and exceeded my initial expectations of how much change could be effected. The scope of the changes was far-reaching and for most of the schools I think the training session opened up various possibilities and helped them on their journey towards quality. One of the schools responded to the 'Dear Phil' letter with little or no promise of action. It was interesting to note that the ancillary alone was present at the course. The message was that all is well and no change is necessary; however the tone of the letter suggested that perhaps this is not the case. One other school had no teacher representative and they too seemed to find it difficult to develop much beyond the sharing of the fictional document. On the other hand, those schools with teacher, ancillary and headteacher present seemed to be able to make the greatest strides, which gives emphasis to the importance of empowerment and team-work.

Reflections on the Process

I was pleasantly surprised by the apparent success of the approach and have already begun to shift the emphasis of my training sessions towards this model. As the title of this chapter suggests, I was not expecting to get it right first time but felt that by being responsive to the feedback I would be able to develop a set of benchmarks which would form the framework for a quality approach to training that was close to the customer and action-biased. I decided to present this as a set of benchmarks against which future training can be measured and evaluated. In keeping with the quality gurus I decided to give them a punchy title – The Ten Training Triggers.

Chapter 15
Number-crunching Quality Control in Teacher Education

Carl Parsons and Keith Sharpe

Introduction

The Higher Education Funding Council for England (HEFCE), the Higher Education Quality Council (HEQC) and the Department for Education (DfE) are sources of explicit external pressure on colleges and universities to be more rigorous and more public in their evaluation systems. Quality assessment (HEFCE) of individual subject areas and quality audit (HEQC) across the institution as a whole require that efficient and thorough-going course monitoring and evaluation are carried out and that the results of these evaluations and follow-up to action points are documented. The University of Central England has a Student Satisfaction Research Unit which has reported on student satisfaction and dissatisfaction since 1989 (SSRU, 1993). Their surveys, using seven-point rating scales, have covered a wide range of institutional life. In their studies they have sampled from amongst the student groups and their report compares measures of satisfaction and importance across faculties and sites.

The pilot exercise reported here, conducted at the end of the summer term 1993, involved collaboration between the Academic Standards Unit and Course Leaders in Teacher Education in the construction or adaptation of questionnaires, handling of the quantitative data and the preparation of a report. *All* students in the courses present on that day were surveyed – except where the tutor forgot! The exercise may be judged by its appropriateness in terms of fulfilling (in part) course evaluation needs, its efficiency in terms of requiring only limited time of both staff and students, and in terms of its utility in providing course managers with information (alongside other data on course quality) relevant to course development.

The following sections illustrate the way a mainly quantitative evaluation of student perceptions and judgements has been managed across the totality of a BA (Ed.) teacher education course.

The Overall Pattern of Quality Control within the Canterbury Christ Church BA (Ed.) degree

There are five key distinctive features of the BA (Ed.) degree course which set it apart from other first degree courses offered at the institution and which pose special problems for the management of quality control:

- it is a four-year course;
- it involves very large student numbers (almost 800);
- it involves large numbers of staff from outside the department of teacher education;
- it involves cooperation with schools and other educational institutions
- it is subject to specific external criteria laid down by the Council for the Accreditation of Teacher Education.

A broad overview of the mechanisms in place for quality control of this organizationally-complex course is shown in Figure 15.1. This is essentially a simple diagrammatic representation of how the planning – monitoring – evaluation cycle is structured institutionally in organized events. Formally arranged student input into the cycle occurs at clearly defined points, notably the three types of meeting

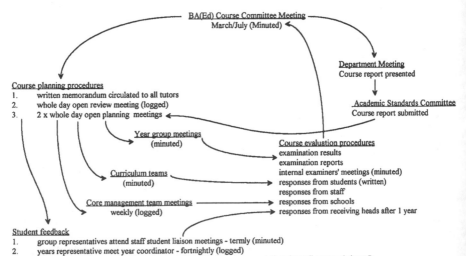

Figure 15.1 Quality control mechanisms within the BA(Ed.) degree

listed under the heading 'student feedback' and the fourth item in the list of course evaluation procedures. The cycle as a whole generates a vast amount of documentation which is then available for quality audit. Qualitative data about student perceptions are in this way already produced in the form of minutes from the 'feedback' meetings. This, taken together with the huge numbers involved, pointed to the need for written evaluative responses from students to be largely quantitative in nature, although some specific decisions still needed to be made.

A number of issues needed to be addressed prior to launching into the pilot: one was whether there should be *some* place for qualitative expression of student perception and if so, what the balance in the questionnaire should be between quantitative and qualitative data; a second was whether the same questionnaire format should be used across all four year-groups or whether each year should have a questionnaire constructed specifically to reflect its particular course content; a third was whether *every* student or a representative sample should be asked for an opinion.

Discussions between the quality review and enhancement officer, the BA (Ed.) course director and the year-group coordinators produced answers to these questions that tended all to point in the same direction. If the qualitative aspect simply took the form of an invitation to write a comment about each course component should the student so wish, with the main focus being on numerical estimation of the value of courses, then it would be possible to survey every student. Aggregating all the numerical assessments for any given course would give it an overall 'value'. Once it was agreed that this was to be done it seemed sensible that it should be done in the same way for all four year-groups.

Setting up the Process

Having decided upon this broad approach it became clear that the number of questions which could be asked was constrained by the need to avoid unmanageable quantities of data. The quality officer and course director reached the conclusion that three main issues needed addressing in relation to each course component:

• Do students judge the component to have provided a quality learning experience?
• Has the component assisted their professional development?
• Has undertaking assignments in connection with the component been valuable?

CANTERBURY CHRIST CHURCH COLLEGE, DEPARTMENT OF TEACHER EDUCATION
BA(Ed) Year 1 Evaluation Questionnaire

For each course component please circle one of the reponses to each of the items below. If you have a comment to make use the space provided. All responses are confidential. They will help the course teams judge the effectiveness of their courses.

English

	Strongly agree	Agree	Disagree	Dis-agree	Strongly disagree
1 The teaching/learning experiences on this aspect of the course are of a high quality	5	4	3	2	1
2 What I have learned in this aspect of the course will be useful in helping me to become a good teacher	5	4	3	2	1
3 Course assignments are appropriate and useful	5	4	3	2	1

Comment:

Mathematics

	Strongly agree	Agree	Disagree	Dis-agree	Strongly disagree
1 The teaching/learning experiences on this aspect of the course are of a high quality	5	4	3	2	1
2 What I have learned in this aspect of the course will be useful in helping me to become a good teacher	5	4	3	2	1
3 Course assignments are appropriate and useful	5	4	3	2	1

Comment:

Science and Technology

	Strongly agree	Agree	Disagree	Dis-agree	Strongly disagree
1 The teaching/learning experiences on this aspect of the course are of a high quality	5	4	3	2	1
2 What I have learned in this aspect of the course will be useful in helping me to become a good teacher	5	4	3	2	1
3 Course assignments are appropriate and useful	5	4	3	2	1

Comment:

School-based work

	Strongly agree	Agree	Disagree	Dis-agree	Strongly disagree
1 The teaching/learning experiences on this aspect of the course are of a high quality	5	4	3	2	1
2 What I have learned in this aspect of the course will be useful in helping me to become a good teacher	5	4	3	2	1
3 Course assignments are appropriate and useful	5	4	3	2	1

Comment:

Information Technology

	Strongly agree	Agree	Disagree	Dis-agree	Strongly disagree
1 The teaching/learning experiences on this aspect of the course are of a high quality	5	4	3	2	1
2 What I have learned in this aspect of the course will be useful in helping me to become a good teacher	5	4	3	2	1

Comment:

Figure 15.2 Example page from evaluation questionnaire

The process of operationalizing this course evaluation procedure involved the following steps:

Step 1. Each of these concerns was turned into a statement to be responded to on a five-point scale. Space was also left for students to comment on each course component. The course components to be evaluated were agreed with each year coordinator. Figure 15.2 gives a sample page from one of the questionnaires.

Step 2. Tutors gave the questionnaire to their groups at a specific time allocated for its completion and then collected them all in. Step 3. Part-time clerical staff were employed to key the data into a lap-top computer. Clerical staff reported that it was much quicker to key the data into the computer than to tally by hand which they had done for other blocks of evaluation data. One hundred questionnaires with 50 digits to be keyed in for each can be carried out in two hours. Step 4. The data file was then read into the VAX and the file set up as an SPSSx file. The setting up of the file and running procedures to extract the data in the form required (e.g., by sub-groups, gender, etc.) can, in most cases, be managed in one hour.

Step 5. The analysis consisted of presenting an analysis for *all* the students across the 5-point scale together with the mean and standard deviation (the mean falling somewhere between 5 and 1). The mean scores were also produced for each *group*. These results were entered on to the original questionnaire which was word-processed to make space and also to leave a gap for comments to be inserted later as these were extracted from student questionnaires. Figure 15.3 gives an example of the BA (Ed.) Year 2 evaluation report produced in this way. An alternative form of presentation of the results is as percentage positive, percentage negative and mean. Figure 15.4 gives an extract produced to this format.

Step 6. The report and the original questionnaires were then handed back to the year-group leader or course coordinator and could be given back to the group tutors. The group tutors were to have the responsibility to extract comments, to review for themselves the quantitative results and then to marshal their own views on the success and quality of the course during the year. Figure 15.5 provides a format for recording staff perceptions and judgements.

SUBJECT Y

	Strongly agree (5)	(4)	(3)	(2)	Strongly disagree (1)
1. The teaching/learning experiences on this aspect of the course are of a high quality.	6	30	42	18	6

	Mean	St Dev	Cases
For entire population	3.12	1.1	112
Group 1	3.25	1.2	11
Group 2	3.27	.8	12
Group 3	3.33	.9	8
Group 4	3.23	1.2	14
Group 5	3.20	1.1	14
Group 6	3.29	1.2	8
Group 7	3.00	1.00	12
Group 8	2.68	.9	15
Group 9	2.50	.8	18
Total Cases = 112			

	Strongly agree (5)	(4)	(3)	(2)	Strongly disagree (1)
2. What I have learned in this aspect of the course will be useful in helping me to become a good teacher.	8	45	29	11	7

	Mean	St Dev	Cases
For entire population	3.35	1.1	110
Group 1	3.36	1.1	10
Group 2	3.54	1.1	12
Group 3	3.80	1.0	8
Group 4	3.57	1.4	14
Group 5	3.46	1.1	13
Group 6	3.64	.9	8
Group 7	3.00	1.2	12
Group 8	2.87	1.0	15
Group 9	2.40	.9	18
Total Cases = 112	Missing Cases = 2 or 1.8 Pct		

	Strongly agree (5)	(4)	(3)	(2)	Strongly disagree (1)
3. Course assignments are appropriate and worthwhile.	16	48	24	8	4

	Mean	St Dev	Cases
For entire population	3.65	1.3	108
Group 1	4.00	1.0	10
Group 2	3.72	1.3	11
Group 3	3.80	1.2	8
Group 4	3.71	1.0	14
Group 5	3.40	1.3	13
Group 6	3.76	.8	8
Group 7	3.30	1.4	12
Group 8	3.50	1.2	15
Group 9	3.80	1.1	17
Total Cases = 112	Missing Cases = 4 or 3.6 Pct		

Figure 15.3 Example 1 of analysed quantitative data

YEAR A

SUBJECT B

1. The teaching/learning experiences on this aspect of
    the course are of a high quality.

	% positive	% negative	Mean	No.
All	32	30	3.0	47
Group 1	25	17	3.2	12
Group 2	59	0	3.6	17
Group 3	11	66	2.2	18

2. What I have learned in this aspect of the course will be
    useful in helping me to become a good teacher.

	% positive	% negative	Mean	No.
All	38	27	3.1	47
Group 1	33	17	3.2	12
Group 2	71	0	3.8	17
Group 3	12	61	2.4	18

3. Course assignments are appropriate and worthwhile.

	% positive	% negative	Mean	No.
All	51	25	3.3	43
Group 1	67	0	3.7	12
Group 2	47	27	3.2	15
Group 3	44	43	3.1	16

    Comment:

SUBJECT C

1. The teaching/learning experiences on this aspect of the
    course are of a high quality.

	% positive	% negative	Mean	No.
All	81	2	4.1	46
Group 1	83	0	4.1	12
Group 2	64	6	3.8	17
Group 3	94	0	4.4	17

2. What I have learned in this aspect of the course will be
    Useful in helping me to become a good teacher.

	% positive	% negative	Mean	No.
All	78	4	4.1	45
Group 1	58	0	3.9	12
Group 2	75	6	4.0	16
Group 3	94	6	4.4	17

    Comment:

Figure 15.4 Example 2 of analysed qualitative data

Tutor:_____

This is a structure you might find helpful but if you prefer something else please use it.

Title of course_____   Year_____

The aspect of the course that went well

The areas of weakness in the course

The changes I think should be made to the course (content, resources, teaching methods, context, assesssment)

Figure 15.5 BA(Ed.) course evaluations. Tutor evaluation of course taught

It should be noted that there are ways of carrying out the analysis using EXCEL and linking a PC to the VAX so that result files, tables, etc. can be imported into the PC and word-processed appropriately as blocks into the original word-processed questionnaire. Secretarial support could be organized to do this relatively cheaply and efficiently.

Staff Discussion of the Evaluation Procedure

As can be seen from Figure 15.1, the main forum for considering the outcomes of this evaluation exercise is the BA (Ed.) course committee meeting. Even prior to this the procedure had sparked off a lot of informal debate and in some cases feelings ran high. Although the reasons for adopting this approach in the context of the BA (Ed.) course were generally understood, some staff expressed reservations about it. Some of these are articulated below.

1. The meaning of the term 'quality' is not self-evident. Students may make assessments of 'quality' on a whole range of different bases: because they liked the lecturer, because the course was easy to follow, because the course was hard to follow, because it was familiar, because it was unfamiliar, because it involved certain types of activity, because it was a subject they always enjoy and so on. In this sense they may not all be assessing the same thing and this undermines the usefulness of aggregated numerical values.

2. Students may not be well placed to measure 'quality'. The value of courses may not be immediately apparent at the time the questionnaire is administered.

3. Similarly, students may not be in a position to assess the usefulness of a course component in helping them to become a good teacher. This may be particularly the case for first-year students whose professional experience is extremely limited.

4. There is a tendency for all questionnaire respondents to 'plump for the middle' unless a course component is perceived to be really good or really bad. The apparent 'scientific accuracy' of the one-place decimal statistics actually masks a rather arbitrary, generalized and vague assessment. In other words, too much store should not be put on the figures.

5. Some tutors felt the comments were the most useful because at least with them it was clear what the student meant.

6. Some of the problems which might underlie low numerical evaluations of course component quality were beyond tutors' control, such as the timetabling of sessions in one year-group

between 4 p.m. and 6 p.m.

7. Asking only three questions about each course component did not provide sufficiently detailed data on which to base future planning of courses.

8. Some staff were unhappy about the invidious comparisons implicit in the numerical values 'earned' by their courses. There was a concern that the process could degenerate into a popularity poll.

9. This process treated all students' responses as equally valid when they may not be. One tutor argued it was unfair that his courses should be assessed by disaffected students or those whose attendance record was poor.

On the positive side, tutors underlined the importance of evaluating courses and appreciated the ease of use of this technique. It was acknowledged that all evaluation procedures have some drawbacks. Some staff were pleasantly surprised by the results for their components and it is important to stress that the overall impression was far from negative. During discussion at the course committee meeting the following points emerged in response to the reservations outlined above.

1. It is true that 'quality' can mean different things, but to say that something has 'quality' is to express a degree of thoughtful, positive approval. This question is after all addressed to an intelligent and successfully educated group within the top 20 per cent of the population as judged by the possession of qualifications. One might wonder at how a student who would assess 'quality' of teaching/learning experiences solely on the whimsical basis of liking for the lecturer could have been selected for teacher training in the first place!

2. and 3. The student perspective is only *one* perspective on the course. On the other hand, it may be that there is room for tutors to be more explicit about why students are being asked to do certain things in a given course component, what the value of the knowledge or skill activity is and why it will promote professional development.

4. While the mental regression towards the mean may be a reality, the actual results did show clearly structured differences. One decimal point may not be very significant but recurring patterns probably are.

5. Qualitative comments are valuable and need to be taken into consideration in conjunction with the quantitative outcomes. There is everything to be gained from using both types of information. Even if it were practically possible there is no guarantee that a purely qualitative procedure would provide a more reliable or accurate

picture. People frame their comments in the context of different perspectives and on the basis of different, and unrevealed, taken-for-granted assumptions. In the event, several course components had contradictory things written about them by different students.

6. There is no doubt that students respond to 'externally determined' conditions such as timetable slots, either positively or negatively. In practice, however, there were still significant differences between the numerical evaluations assigned to different components subject to the same timetabling constraints.

7. It would have been difficult in this approach to ask more than three questions. The qualitative comments do provide some detail to assist future planning.

8. The comparisons need not be invidious in a personalized sense. They can equally be regarded as an occasion to reflect on what underlies the differences with a view to improving the course. It has perhaps also to be faced that this kind of differential value assessment is becoming more and more part of the culture of higher, and indeed, all education.

9. It would be difficult to imagine instituting any kind of 'means-test' system whereby only 'worthy' students could be asked for their opinion. There is in any case surely no necessary link between poor attendance and low evaluations; students may feel they benefited from the sessions they attended and may not have felt that about the ones they missed!

Analysing and Interpreting the Data

The person writing the report should draw out the main points to be addressed while still allowing colleagues to scrutinize the data themselves. It is important that in an evaluation review meeting the strong and weak points are identified and action is formulated in relation to evaluation evidence. Below are some examples that arise from a brief examination of Figures 15.3 and 15.4.

Looking at the extract presented in Figure 15.3 with the 3.5 quality standard in mind (see the second point in the list below, on the view from the course managers), it is evident that, over all, Subject Y has achieved this with four groups in relation to 2, *useful in helping me to become a good teacher,* and for almost all in relation to 3, *assignments.* In terms of 1, *quality of teaching/learning experiences,* no groups achieved the quality standard.

Where a group scores more than 0.5 below the mean for the Year, this could be a prompt for further investigation and action. Groups 8 and 9 fall into this category for items 1 and 2. For Subject Y, the assignments evoke a more positive response than is the case with most other subjects (not shown here). This being the case, it may be worthwhile looking for ways of communicating what makes assignments more highly appreciated for this subject with a view to replicating these characteristics in the assessment tasks of other subjects.

Figure 15.3 sets out the tables with standard deviation included. In some cases the 'spread' that this statistic measures can be helpful; in this case the variability is not great and one would need to exercise caution where the number of cases is small.

In Figure 15.4 the 'spread' is shown by reporting per cent positive and negative as well as the mean. It is starkly clear here that Subject C is well received; Subject B seems to require attention.

The View from Course Managers

The evidence provided by quantitative student evaluation data has proved useful in the following ways:

- These data offer an overall picture of the course, albeit an abstracted and simplified one from one perspective.
- One can establish benchmarks for mean scores; 3.5 *could* be set as the quality standard, with anything less triggering consideration of steps for improvement. Mean scores are given in the report, part of which is presented in Figure 15.2 but, as an alternative, the per cent positive and per cent negative can be set out as in Figure 15.3.
- The mean scores or per cent positive allow a comparison of course components and of groups. These comparisons may be regarded as invidious or as inevitable and starkly, helpfully, provocative.
- In some subject areas it *appears* to be easier than in others to be judged successful and useful by students. For most subjects or course components there is no intrinsic reason for low scores. Where they occur one is prompted to look for reasons and to ask why the component could not receive as high a score as other similar parts of the course.
- This process encourages staff to develop their own perspective on course quality and motivates them to contribute to the discussion about it.
- Individuals and course components which are judged successful should be examined to see what it is that makes for their success (almost certainly not mere popularity). Steps should be taken to

share successful methodology and course management.
- Individuals and courses being judged less positively may need help to improve.
- Despite the disadvantage that only three questions are asked, these data reveal patterned regularities in student perception of course quality which can inform the drawing-up of action plans to improve course provision in subsequent years.

Following-up Student Evaluation Questionnaire Analysis

Our learners are mature and intelligent and have a valid perspective on the experience they have had during the year; they have a valid view on 'whether the course is helping me to become a good teacher' and on whether teaching and learning experience are 'of a high quality'. What they have to say has to be taken seriously.

Tutors also have a valid perspective on the courses which they have organized and taught. Course evaluations should not be dominated by student opinion. Staff should marshal their own thoughts and evaluations on a course and where possible document these.

Equal consideration should be given to the assessed attainment of students. Altogether one has student opinion, staff opinion, student results and examiners' reports to inform an evaluation of the course. The best way of utilizing evaluation data is as follows:

- Student evaluation data are analysed and an appropriately condensed report is produced. This should include selected quotes from the open-ended parts of the questionnaire.
- One member of the teaching group is given a task of drafting *action points* or identifying issues.
- Individual members of staff set down in writing *their* perceptions and judgements about the course or the part of it which they taught.
- Staff who have taught the course or who will be teaching it next year come together for a *one-hour* meeting which is tightly and robustly chaired and has the remit of considering the draft action points, amending, deleting or adding as the group sees fit, and deciding what action will actually be taken. Documentary preparation for the meeting is vital.
- The *action points* and the *responses* to them are recorded and filed (and acted upon). They are a key part of the evaluation for the following year.
- Central to the whole exercise is the improvement in practice,

raising the attainment of our students and maximizing the quality of the provision made for our 'customers'.

• As part of the continuing cycle of course evaluation those areas of a course judged weak should be monitored in the first term of the next year. A date and method should be decided for this and set out in the action plan; it is important that a year is not left to pass before ascertaining if necessary improvement has taken place.

• All reports and reviews should be compiled with care and filed. They now form part of the evidence that a department manages its quality assurance effectively.

Conclusion

Having done it once, with considerable professional and course improvement value, the student questionnaires are being used again in 1994. This time the aim is to extract as much value from their use as before, but with less effort. The undertaking can be streamlined and written reports will be briefer, though debate may take longer. The action planning that follows from it all will receive more attention because that is what drives practical course improvement.

Chapter 16
Training for Quality Management in Healthcare

Hugh C H Koch

Quality Improvement in Healthcare: The Context

This chapter addresses training issues in relation to quality improvement in the health service, predominantly in the UK, but also with occasional reference to health services in other parts of the world. Many of the issues raised and discussed have relevance for other public sector services, such as education (see Chesterton, Chapter 3, this volume), and are in fact currently being applied in those settings.

Healthcare has been the focus of considerable attention, not only recently, but for many decades, from governments and the public alike. The British NHS is seen worldwide as a provider of high quality healthcare and service, meeting if not exceeding the six

Figure 16.1 Dimensions of quality in healthcare (from Maxwell, 1984)

160

dimensions of quality outlined in Maxwell's (1984) seminal paper, namely access to services, relevance and equity, efficiency of service, acceptability to patient, and effectiveness of service (see Figure 16.1).

Since 1989, many provider healthcare units and some purchasers have been developing organized quality management systems to ensure not only that quality of care and service exist, but that it is continuously improving. The many and varied efforts in this direction are usually given the overall label 'Total Quality Management'. This approach to managing successful healthcare delivery systems is well documented elsewhere (Koch, 1991a, 1992b) and it is recommended that the reader refer to these texts for in-depth detail. A brief diagrammatic illustration of what constitutes a TQM approach is shown in Figures 16.2 and 16.3. Minor amendments to the wording

Figure 16.2 TQM in healthcare

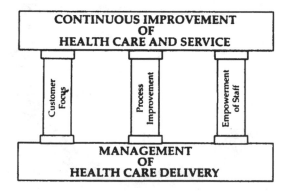

Figure 16.3 The pillars of quality

in both of these figures would enable them to fit any other public service. TQM for any enterprise involves:

- quality improvement culture
- customer focus
- team work
- process improvement
- quality improvement
- staff empowerment
- tools and techniques

The training implication of these will be addressed in a later section of this chapter. Each of these components needs to exist in a hospital, community service or primary care team, (or school and college or university) to ensure customer requirements are met, as illustrated in Figure 16.4.

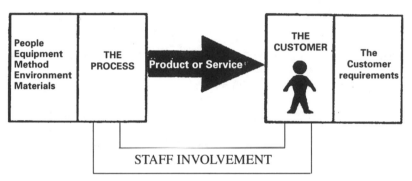

Figure 16.4 Staff involvement in identifying and satisfying customer needs

Underpinning all of this is the need for a provider unit and *all* its staff to hold and share a set of core quality values. These are shown in Figure 16.5 and seem self-explanatory – experience suggests that different levels of understanding and application exist.

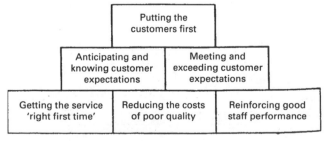

Figure 16.5 Core values of TQM

So where do we go from here? Some provider units at this stage would embark on a structured and well-thought-out 'Implementation plan' without fully understanding the need to train for quality improvement. These areas are:

- definitions of quality
- understanding TQM
- integration of TQM and business planning
- TQM policy and strategy development
- TQM and non-clinical support functions
- process improvement
    - audits
    - outcome management
    - quality costs and cost-effectiveness
    - external accreditation
    - problem-solving
    - flow-charting
- top management leadership of TQM
- staff involvement in TQM
- quality systems and systems auditing
- benchmarking
- maintaining momentum in TQM.

A comprehensive training programme to support the initiation, full

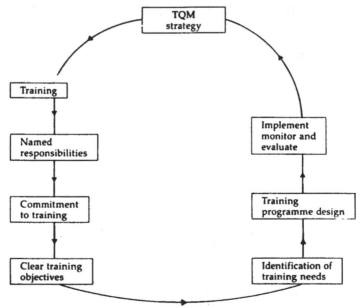

Figure 16.6 The quality training cycle

implementation and sustaining of a TQM programme would need to address all eleven of these areas, within a quality training cycle illustrated in Figure 16.6.

Stages of TQM and Training Requirements

In a recent TQM healthcare text (Koch, 1992b), an implementation chart illustrated the several stages of TQM from strategy development to maintaining momentum; this chart is reproduced in Figure 16.7.

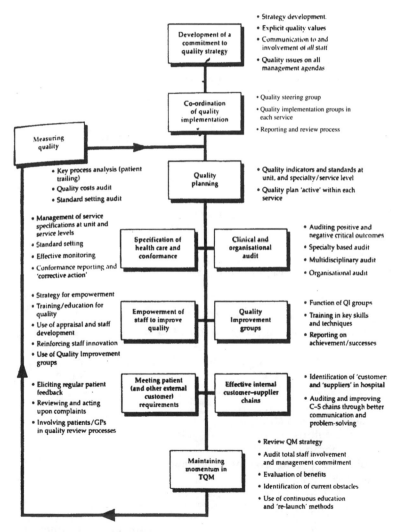

Figure 16.7 Quality implementation chart

Each major part of this process has its own particular training requirements, especially the four major planks of TQM referred to in Figure 16.3, namely:

- customer focus
- process improvement
- staff empowerment
- management and coordination of TQM, leading to continuous improvement.

Alongside these 'technical' areas, key areas of management development for quality improvement which have their own training requirements are:

- developing a quality culture and commitment
- improving teamwork
- quality improvement tools and techniques.

These will be taken in turn in the subsequent section.

Developing a Quality Improvement Culture and Commitment

Leadership and *firing on all cylinders*
Gaining staff commitment Part I: *Aren't we committed already?*
Vision of quality
    Putting the patient first (and other customers first)
    Meeting and exceeding patient expectations
    Getting the service *right first time*
    Reducing the costs of poor quality
    Reinforcing good staff performance
Outlining the strategy
Who's involved in developing the strategy?
Overcoming potential obstacles
    Lack of top management commitment and vision
    'Flavour of the month/year' attitudes
    Hospital/community service culture and management style
    Poor appreciation of TQM concepts, principles and practices
    Lack of structure for TQM activities
    Medical uninvolvement
    Managers or administrators
Where is your culture now?
Gaining staff commitment Part II
    Ten point checklist for quality communication
Planning implementation
Integration of TQM with business planning
Would you get the European Quality Award yet?

Figure 16.8 Gaining and sustaining staff commitment: developing a strategy

Koch (1992a) listed the main issues in gaining and sustaining staff commitment; these are reproduced in Figure 16.8. The reader is referred to this text for detail. Training is specifically required to address two key issues: total staff involvement in developing and understanding the strategy; and addressing common obstacles to getting commitment to TQM.

The word 'total' in TQM predominantly refers to the need to ensure *all* staff know and understand what the strategy and vision for continuous quality improvement in the organization is – whether it be a hospital, community service or general practice. Training needs to be available to cascade TQM expertise and capability from top management to all operational staff, as Figure 16.9 illustrates.

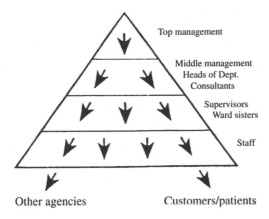

Figure 16.9 Cascading TQM

Dale (1993) identified the top 21 difficulties in getting commitment to TQM in any organization; these are shown in Figure 16.10. Each of these was prioritised by his research group of organizations in terms of relative difficulty . Training would need to address the capability to overcome these inevitable obstacles in terms of:

- increasing quality improvement behaviour and attitudes;
- linking individual and organizational objectives in the short- and long-term;
- prevention not treatment approach to problems
- clarity of responsibilities and roles;
- cross-departmental liaison and cooperation;
- quality management skills, tools and techniques (see later section);
- abilities to identify and release 'failure' costs.

Changing behaviour and attitudes
Emphasis on short-term objectives
A tendency to cure symptoms of a problem
Production schedules and costs are treated as main priorities
Employees are not sure what is required of them
Barriers between departments
Managers are not sure what is required of them
Lack of objectives and strategies
Quality system based on detection not prevention
Lack of expertise in quality management
A lack of resources
A lack of intellectual thought given to the subject
Quality management tools are seen as an end in themselves
Uncertainty about what to do next
Fear
Quality improvement is the concern of the quality department
Quality improvement is the concern of production
A lack of top management commitment
Conflict between production and quality department
Over reliance on the quality manual
SPC is the answer to all problems

Figure 16.10 Twenty-one difficulties in getting commitment to TQM (from Dale, 1993)

Developing a quality-conscious culture and commitment needs coordination via a clear organizational structure which illustrates how quality management is coordinated and how it supports the line management structure. Key elements which need to be linked are: directorate (or its equivalent); quality steering group; quality improvement teams; and quality department (if it exists). The ability to understand organizational issues often requires training in the middle management and medical groups.

Improving Teamwork

In large healthcare organizations with clear management structures, most if not all staff work on a day-to-day basis in operational teams, either uni-professional (e.g., ward nursing team) or multi-disciplinary (e.g., community mental health team; theatre team). Few staff have ever received training in effective teamwork covering such areas as:

- team communication;
- conflict resolution;
- using team members' strengths;
- understanding of professional roles;

• benefits of team (as compared to individual) effort.

Key areas for training in addition to the above are:

- • liaison between medical staff and other groups;
- • liaison between clinical and support staff groups;
- • managers' awareness of clinical quality issues and conflicts.

Within the context of quality management, four types of quality team are likely to be found working and in need of their own development and training. These are the *Quality Improvement Steering Group* – the senior 'driving force' for TQM, accountable to the chief executive and board; the *Quality Action Team* – a subset of the QI Steering Group, spending more time and effort in providing expertise and support to the line managers and clinicians; the *Clinical Audit Group* – the 'driving force' for medical and clinical audit, often being a 'collection' of interested clinicians needing direction and training to fully utilize their enthusiasm and skills; and the *Quality Improvement Teams* – multi-disciplinary cross-functional teams at an operational level, problem solving and cutting through bureaucracy and traditional practices which don't work.

Quality Improvement Tools and Techniques

The most straightforward aspect of 'training for quality' is to make available training in the main tools and techniques for quality improvement. These are:

- • process analysis and flow-charting
- • cause and effect analysis
- • use of data and graphical presentation
- • clinical care pathways/collaborative care planning and audit
- • provision of patient information
- • eliciting and acting on patient feedback
- • customer care and courtesy
- • appraisal and personal development planning
- • communication with staff
- • quality improvement teamwork.

These are fully described in Koch (1991a, 1992b). Training in each specific technique with back-up paperwork is necessary here.

Training Methods

Several different approaches for training in TQM currently exist:

Internal: 1. Workshops
               2. Seminars
               3. Briefings
External: 1. Qualification courses
                  Conceptual and information based
                  Action-learning and skills based
               2. Short courses workshops
                  General training methods
                  Skills based
                  Case study based
                  Attitude changing
               3. Simulation workshops
               4. Training company task force.

Internal training needs to be linked and tailored to the overall quality and business strategy of the unit. Several high quality healthcare-specific training packages are now available to support the trainer in providing effective sessions (Koch 1991b, 1992a, 1993, 1994). These could be adapted for mainstream education institutions. External training opportunities are available via the various Health Service Management Centres (e.g., Birmingham, Manchester, Leeds) and other independent consultancy and training companies and publishers.

Sustaining Momentum via Training

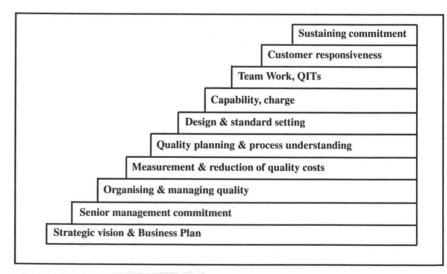

Figure 16.11 Building blocks of TQM

It is said that TQM is relatively easy to establish and extremely difficult to sustain in any organization, not least healthcare provider
units. Trainers and quality managers alike need continually to
monitor the extent to which key staff have mastered the 'building
blocks' of TQM illustrated in Figure 16.11.

Updating and further training for new and existing staff needs to
be available using both internal and external training resources. Of
the many adages about implementing TQM, one of the most relevant
is: 'the search for excellence rests on the effectiveness of the staff
training throughout the organization'.

Chapter 17
Strategic Quality Improvement at De Montfort University

Philip Cox

The Background Context

Within the framework of post-binary structures established following the 1991 White Paper on higher education, a lively and at times contentious debate has taken place as to the meaning of quality within higher education, with a number of different conceptual approaches vying for recognition as the dominant paradigm (Barnett, 1992; Harvey and Green, 1993).

From within this debate, the De Montfort University[1] has conducted a major review of its quality management systems with a view to developing a strategic approach to quality maintenance and enhancement, in ways which reflect the aspirations (and constraints) of the University and the perceived needs and expectations of external 'stakeholders'.

It was evident from the outset of this review that pursuance of principles to underpin a 'fitness for purpose' approach to quality would require significant organizational and cultural changes from the traditions for quality assurance established under the aegis of the Council for National Academic Awards (CNAA). A brief overview of this 'agenda for change' is given in the following section.

Strategic Quality Improvement – Key Principles

1. *Explicitly stated objectives for a quality service and related performance standards.* A first reflection on the principle of fitness for purpose must address the question, 'whose purposes?'. In recognition of a shift from a provider-centred to a more customer-centred view of quality, it is evident that agreements must be established for reconciling the goals, capabilities and constraints of the providing

institution, and the diverse needs and expectations of various client groups and regulatory bodies. Through the formulation of learning contracts or institutional charters, it is possible to establish a framework for agreement on the objectives and standards for a quality service, based on a view of quality as 'consistently meeting agreed customer needs'.

Strategies must also be developed for ensuring alignment between quality objectives at all levels of an institution if common purpose is to be secured. This means that corporate objectives must be translated into terms which are meaningful (i.e., operational) at a local level. It also means that objectives must be negotiated, not imposed, if common ownership is to be established.

2. *Planned and appropriately documented activities for achieving the quality objectives.* Effective quality management requires a shift of emphasis from a detection mode (have we done the job correctly?) to a prevention mode (are we capable of doing the job correctly and do we continue to do the job correctly?) (Oakland, 1990).

Application of the principles of quality planning and management poses some difficulties within higher education. Documented quality systems, which define the structures, processes and resources for achieving the objectives set, must be developed in ways which provide adequate confidence (assurance) that given requirements for quality will be satisfied without the high level of prescribed control evident in industrial quality systems (Burrows *et al.,* 1992). Students may, for example, seek and expect consistency of performance (compliance with agreed protocols for the marking and return of course assignments) *and* flexibility of approach (adaption of teaching and learning strategies to the evolving needs of individual students).

Within British higher education, course validation arrangements have sought to establish the capability of new courses in relation to stated design requirements and threshold quality standards, though subsequent adherence to the design specifications of the approved course scheme remains problematic.

3. *Provision for the ongoing monitoring and evaluation of performance against agreed objectives and standards.* A level of rigour in performance monitoring has not always been evident in performance evaluation.[2] Evaluation should be primarily concerned with exploring the relationships between intentions and outcomes (i.e., effectiveness in the achievement of agreed objectives), though 'normative' yardsticks may also be used as part of the evaluation

process (i.e., comparative national benchmarks and time-series data). Perceived deficiencies in evaluation may be attributed to a lack of clarity in defining educational objectives.

Within British higher education, monitoring and evaluation have been conceived essentially as end-inspection activities, based on annual (or five-yearly) reporting exercises. By contrast, under a preventative strategy, monitoring and evaluation should become ongoing activities concerned with eliminating the causes of unsatisfactory performance at relevant stages in the educational cycle. This follows the British Standards Institute's definition of quality control as 'operational techniques and activities aimed at monitoring a process and eliminating causes of unsatisfactory performance at relevant stages of the quality loop' (BSI, 1990).

4. *Establishment of clear protocols for action where performance falls below agreed objectives/standards (quality maintenance) or to facilitate a systematic improvement in the quality of provision (quality enhancement).* Performance monitoring and evaluation are too often undertaken for retrospective rather than developmental purposes. Evaluation exercises should be forward-looking and concerned with the needs and opportunities for systematic quality improvement.

Studies in quality management confirm the merits of pursuing a focused and in-depth approach to performance monitoring and evaluation based on agreement as to the priorities for quality improvement. Such priorities, or 'critical success factors', should be identified by reference to perceived needs at different levels within the organizational structure. Improvement plans should, in turn, identify 'critical processes' i.e., the key activities which must be successfully undertaken to achieve the objectives set.

Finally, effective protocols must be developed for reporting on and reviewing the outcomes of performance monitoring and evaluation. The resolution of quality problems will frequently extend beyond the authority or control of those mandated to undertake self-evaluation exercises and the willingness/ability of managers to address reported problems will do much to inspire staff confidence in the effectiveness of quality systems. Recognition of opportunities for staff to inform strategic decision making will also act to reinforce a sense of common ownership.

Principles into Practice – The Course Log

The aforementioned principles can be applied to products, services or activities at any organizational level. At the De Montfort University, a framework for operationalizing these principles has been established through redefined protocols for the validation and ongoing review of taught courses of study. This section will outline how, in order to address the 'agenda for change' described in the previous section, a fundamental reorientation of the course review process has been effected through the mechanism of an instrument known as the 'course log'.[3]

Confirmation of Agreed Objectives

In pursuit of a strategy for 'process control', all course teams are required to undertake a series of 'formative reviews' at defined stages within an academic session. Each review looks at particular aspects of course provision and performance, appropriate to that stage in the academic cycle. The following stages in the review cycle have been identified for this purpose (modifiable for semester-based programmes):

1. Student access   First term
2. Course management and resources   Second term
3. Course structure and delivery   Third term
4. Course outcomes   First term (following
                                          session)

Within the course log, an extensive range of quality criteria and indicators have been defined and classified in relation to these four stages in the review cycle, covering course operations from initial marketing to alumni matters. Such a span reflects a concern with quality as the '*totality* of features and characteristics of a product or service that bear on its ability to satisfy stated or implied needs' (BSI, 1990).

The quality criteria/indicators have been drawn from a wide range of internal and external sources, including institutional policy statements. The use of institutional policy statements as the basis for reflecting on and formulating course policy objectives is consistent with one of the key aims of the University's revised approach to quality management, namely that there should be a greater awareness of the University's mission, policies and strategic objectives and how these are reflected in school, departmental and course planning.

As the first stage in each review exercise, course teams are asked to confirm in the relevant section of the log agreed course objectives with respect to the identified range of quality criteria/indicators;

instances where the criteria/indicators are considered to be irrelevant to the context of a course; and aspects of course policy not identified within the pre-defined range of criteria/indicators.

The quality criteria and indicators are not intended to be set as final, definitive statements, but simply as starting points in an institutional debate about the setting of explicit objectives and standards for a quality service and how these might be legitimately reconciled at different levels within the institution to ensure a coherent, integrated approach to corporate planning and development.

Performance Monitoring and Evaluation

Within the course log, for each stage of the review cycle, a 'performance profile' is provided for course teams to record data on performance against a subset range of quantitative indicators. Alongside the monitored records of actual performance (and previously identified performance standards/targets where already determined), provision exists for the recording of comparative data identifying trends in course performance (time-series data) and national benchmarks (national data on the performance of cognate higher education courses). Appropriate provision is also made for the recording of information on the more qualitative aspects of performance as obtained in feedback from staff, students, employers, external examiners, etc.

Course teams are asked to evaluate their performance against agreed policy objectives and standards and where appropriate in relation to time-series data and national benchmarks. The appropriateness of course objectives in relation to institutional criteria is also appraised. As part of the evaluation process, course teams are asked to rate their provision and performance using a five-point scale. Such self-evaluation ratings are intended to assist course teams in the process of arriving at collective judgements as to the quality of existing provision and in determining priorities for quality improvement.

Improvement Plans

Measures to maintain or enhance the quality of course provision are recorded within the log. Such records will identify the actions to be undertaken (and by whom), the time-scales involved and the resource implications.

Improvement plans may include changes to agreed objectives, the setting of new performance targets or simply revised systems for achieving the objectives/standards set. Improvement proposals which extend beyond the immediate authority or control of the school are notified to the relevant authority and details entered in the course log.

The course log provides an ongoing record of course operations and a framework for facilitating continuous quality improvement. Actions on problematic issues can be taken as they arise rather than waiting until the end of the review cycle. From information collected as part of the cycle of formative reviews, course teams are expected to complete a synoptic 'course review summary'. This provides an overall appraisal of course operations for the session under review and a summary record of actions taken and proposed. The course review summary is normally completed concurrently with the review of 'course outcomes'.

Following each stage in the review cycle, information from the relevant section of the log is submitted for consideration at school and institutional levels. School reviews are expected to examine course provision and performance in accordance with fitness-for-purpose principles and to identify issues requiring further attention at course, school or institution levels, including possible changes to agreed objectives and plans. Commentaries on the outcomes of course and school review exercises are in turn prepared to inform the processes of planning and review at institutional level.

The Course Log in Operation – An Initial Assessment

Within the De Montfort University, it was recognized from the outset that the implementation of the course log would be an evolutionary process, both in terms of gaining staff understanding and acceptance of new quality management principles, and in terms of the acknowledged need for changes in infrastructure support for course monitoring and evaluation.

The first full cycle of the course review process has now been completed. Course teams and other staff have generally approached this exercise with an open mind: the analysis and evaluation of course provision and performance being undertaken in a thoughtful and generally self-critical manner. A wide range of improvement needs have been identified and addressed at relevant levels within the organizational structure.

Feedback on the general principles underpinning the design and use of the course log has generally been positive, though 'cultural' sensitivities remain on two important aspects of current policy. First, it was anticipated from the outset that the identification of explicit criteria for quality would not readily be accepted by those who subscribe to a 'know it when you see it' view of quality. Internal and external imperatives to define, measure and evaluate quality are an inevitable consequence of any system for quality assessment which requires evidence of claimed quality standards in relation to specifically defined *objectives* for a quality service. Some staff (a minority) continue to view this as a reductionist approach to quality.

Second, concerns have also been expressed regarding the relationship between self-improvement and audit exercises. Whilst the intended role of the course log in promoting ongoing self-evaluation has generally been acknowledged and welcomed, there is an evident danger that the reporting protocols necessarily associated with the use of the log may engender a 'compliance' culture (submitting reports by agreed deadlines) or a culture which undermines critical self-scrutiny (based on fears regarding the possible misuse of self-evaluations as part of internal or external quality assessment/audit exercises).

Critical, if constructive, feedback has also been received on a number of operational problems associated with the use of the course log, most notably the capacity of the institutional information support systems to provide early access to data to support judgements on a much wider range of quality indicators than has hitherto been the case.[4] This matter is currently under review at institutional level and is linked to the provision of an electronic course log which has now been made available to support the recording and transfer of course review information.

The issue of information support is illustrative of a wider organizational issue, namely the capacity of the wider institutional system to respond to issues which fall beyond the authority and control of course teams. Whilst responsibilities and lines of communication are clearly defined within the overall quality systems, it is clear that the willingness of senior managers to address and take action on reported problems will be crucial in developing staff confidence in these systems.

Finally, some staff concerns have been expressed over the costs of quality management exercises, including the opportunity costs associated with competing demands on staff time. Such concerns may reflect a failure to incorporate such activities as integral, properly resourced, elements of course operations at the design stage. More fundamentally, such feedback reveals the need to further demonstrate the high costs of *quality mismanagement* – the quality losses which result from client dissatisfaction and the failure to make optimal use of human, learning and financial resources.

Despite significant initial success, it is recognized that further work is necessary to demonstrate potential benefits and to strengthen staff ownership and commitment to the new quality systems. In response to this situation, activities associated with the future use of the course log will include:

- reinforcing the role of the course log as a self-evaluation instrument (addressing questions which are intrinsic to course quality rather than extraneous form-filling);
- allowing course teams to concentrate on 'focus topics' which are directly relevant to their own needs and priorities or those identified within school or institutional strategic plans;
- reinforcing the role of each school in reviewing the outcomes of course monitoring and evaluation (at relevant stages of the academic cycle);
- enhancing protocols for reporting on matters which fall beyond the authority and control of the school, together with closer monitoring of follow-up action taken in response to issues raised;
- strengthening selective audit functions which assess the effectiveness of operations (including review arrangements) at course, school and institutional levels.

The Course Log – An Overview

The course log provides a framework wherein course objectives with respect to a comprehensive range of operations are more clearly articulated in relation to institutional goals, defined through a range of quality criteria and indicators. It provides for the systematic recording of quantitative and qualitative performance data and for the evaluation of performance based on both criteria- and norm-referencing. It promotes course development through the pursuit of focused quality improvement strategies which are planned and documented.

The course log is based on a review schedule which facilitates corrective action at relevant stages in the academic cycle. It provides a framework for review and development at school and institutional levels through clearly defined protocols for reporting on course outcomes.

More generally, the course log seeks to promote a bottom-up

approach to quality management through the enhancement of staff ownership and responsibility for the quality of education provision, within a strategic framework which ensures that staff, at all levels, are duly accountable for the pursuit of quality goals which are consistent with the overall objectives of the University and the needs and expectations of its client groups.

Footnotes

1. Formerly Leicester Polytechnic, the De Montfort University is a large multi-site institution (over 18,000 registered students) based at Leicester and Milton Keynes with future locations planned at Bedford and Lincoln. An extensive network of franchised and associate college operations has also been established.

2. Performance monitoring refers to the ongoing process of collecting qualitative and quantitative data about a product, service or activity. Performance evaluation refers to the process of drawing conclusions from and making judgements about data collected from the monitoring process.

3. An instrument of the same title developed by the Hertfordshire LEA quality team provided some formative influences in the early development of the DMU model.

4. Staff acceptance of the relevance of such indicators, confirmed as part of the feedback process, suggests that the log has not created a data problem; it has highlighted an existing information deficiency and an improvement need.

Chapter 18

Southampton's Departmental Self-assessment Programme: Success of an Experiment

Robert Green

A Brief History

In the early 1980s and with great foresight, the then vice-chancellor set in train discussions about quality assurance in the University of Southampton. These led, after reports from working parties and after discussion with the local branch of the Association of University Teachers, to the establishment of a joint committee of senate and council for the Assessment of Departmental Academic Performance (ADAP), which was charged with the implementation of a programme of departmental self-assessment. Wisely and deliberately, progress was slow: two 'pilot' studies (of history and chemistry) were undertaken in 1986/7, followed in 1987/8 by a further six 'prototype' assessments. Much was learned from these initial eight assessments and in 1989 the University was ready to embark on a full-scale programme of self-assessment for all its academic and medical departments in our eight faculties (Arts, Education, Engineering, Law, Mathematics, Social Sciences, Science, plus a faculty of Medicine on a separate campus at the city's General Hospital). The joint committee was chaired by a deputy vice-chancellor and from the outset included representatives of senate and lay members of council, thus ensuring that academic members of staff as well as the institution's external laity were fully involved in the development of the scheme. This is not a mere procedural nicety: I shall argue that the success of the University's ADAP programme is crucially bound up with academics' sense of 'ownership' and also with the very real involvement of lay councillors – retired business-people, academics and educational administrators – who have been able to bring to bear a variety of invaluable external perspectives.

By 1989, then, the University had developed and refined the methodology for a programme of quality assurance that was based upon departmental self-assessment. To take the programme further and to reach out to the remaining 40 or so departments, the central administration had to be strengthened and so the academic registrar's department recruited an administrator charged, for a large part of his working week, with providing support for the development of the ADAP programme. (The University chose to appoint me. I combined 20 years' academic experience with some administrative experience, the former, it was perhaps hoped, to give a measure of 'street credibility' in the perception of those senior academics with whom I would be collaborating in the extension of the programme.)

In the next four years progress was rapid and by the end of the present academic year (1993/4) the University will have completed assessment of all its non-medical departments and most of its medical departments at the General Hospital – some 40 assessments in total. In addition, seven 'review' assessments of those departments originally assessed in 1986/8 as pilots or prototypes have been completed and these will be followed by a rolling programme of review assessments in the next few years. The original methodology was designed for the assessment of academic and medical departments but this has now been developed as a tool for the assessment of 'service' and administrative departments: 1991/2 saw a pilot assessment of one of the former (computing services) and in the current year we shall be running pilot assessments of two administrative departments (personnel and the careers advisory service).

In future the assessment of academic departments is planned as part of a four/five year cycle, corresponding if possible to the rhythm of the English Funding Council (HEFCE) and its programme for the assessment of teaching quality in English universities. This HEFCE exercise, which will doubtless soon 'inform' that part of the funding of English universities which relates to the provision of undergraduate teaching, in much the same way as funding for research has for several years been related to the outcomes of the Council's assessment of research quality, makes great demands upon departments being assessed in terms of the documentation required and the preparation of a ten-page statement. Thus it is crucially important that the requirements of the University's internal QA mechanism be, as far as possible, congruent with such external requirements as the HEFCE's and, for certain departments in the faculties of Engineering and Social Sciences, those of external accreditation agencies, such as, for example, the Engineering Council.

At this point, as the initial assessment of academic departments draws to a close and as we extend the scheme to embrace service and administrative departments, it is timely to take stock of what has been achieved and how we might move forward. The success of the self-assessment programme can be measured in two ways, from both external and internal evidence. Externally, the CVCP's Academic Audit Unit, which visited the University early in 1991, found it to be 'an example of good practice in how a university might develop and implement departmental reviews. We congratulate', the auditors continued, 'the University for the careful way in which this searching means of reviewing academic quality has been introduced, refined and for the success with which it has secured the acceptance and support of staff' (CCVP, 1991). The final words of that sentence are indicative of the second means of assessing its success: that, notwithstanding the variety of new, external pressures under which academics have had to operate in the last few years, they have accepted and indeed welcomed the University's own internal procedures. Indeed there have been a number of cases where groupings in the university have actually gone so far as to invite the joint committee to organize a self-assessment outside of the normal schedule of assessments. (Most assessments to date, as we have seen, have been of departments, but in April 1993 the faculty of Medicine, at its own request, undertook self-assessment, requesting that particular attention be paid to the revised BM curriculum for whose composition and delivery it is itself entirely responsible; and to its relationship with the NHS.)

Nevertheless, it is fair to say that academic acceptance of the programme was not won easily or immediately. That the ADAP process is now so much a part of the institutional landscape is attributable to the strong academic membership of the joint committee and to the even-handedness with which the various assessments have been conducted. Self-assessment at the University of Southampton is not perceived as yet another means by which an overbearing managerial class imposes itself upon a sullen lumpenproletariat of lecturers and researchers.

The Process: Profile, Panel, Visit and Report

From the outset the University had been determined that the scheme should be transparent and subject to external verification. Once a department has been selected for assessment in a particular session, usually on the advice of the relevant dean, it sets up its own 'team' of two or three members whose task it is to assemble and edit the 'profile', the department's own self-assessment document. The length and contents of these documents are specified in the 'Notes of guidance', revised periodically and published by the joint committee, and will typically contain material upon the department's teaching activities (including any postgraduate courses, any continuing education work and any 'service' teaching that it 'sells' to another department); its research, publications and consultancy work; and its management and organizational structures. It is also asked to furnish relevant comparative data from those departments in other universities regarded as cognate. Production of the 'profile' is the most onerous part of the exercise and we are now careful to ensure that its contents overlap with the data required by both the periodic research selectivity exercises and the HEFCE's more recent assessments of teaching quality. In order to maintain the loyalty of academic members of staff it is vital that the joint committee is responsive to other external demands being made upon academics and is able to modify its own procedures in order to avoid any assessment overload.

At the same time as a department is preparing its 'profile' against an assessment in perhaps nine months' time, it is asked to submit to the vice-chancellor names of, and brief 'biodata' upon two or three potential candidates to serve as the external adviser. Typically, these are very senior British academics who possess a wide knowledge of their academic field and may, for example, have served upon an HEFCE research panel or have chaired their own academic associations. External advisers are absolutely vital to the health and transparency of the process, for it is their wisdom and neutrality that assures the value of the report that will be written upon the department undertaking assessment. The keystone of the assessment process is the visit to the department of the assessment panel and this will normally occupy one to two days, depending upon the size of the department and whether it is an initial assessment or a review assessment some five years after the former. As well as the external adviser, the panel will comprise a chair, who is normally either an academic member of the joint committee, a lay member of council or a former deputy vice-chancellor; the head of the department under assessment; the dean of the faculty or a nominated deputy; a professorial representative of another faculty; a lay member of council, where that body has not already provided the chair; and a secretary, who will be recruited from the University's central administration.

In advance of the visit the panel will have been provided with the departmental 'profile' and any associated appendices. Other material, such as departmental publications, recruitment literature, folders of material about undergraduate/postgraduate courses and course reviews, will be tabled for the attention of the panel, as will copies of the curricula vitae of academic members of staff. The latter, it should be said, are the only section of the paperwork that does not enter the public domain since the assessment is conceived to be of 'the department' rather than of any individual member thereof. (The University has, of course, a quite separate programme of annual staff appraisal.) During the two-day visit the panel will meet with a cross-section of the whole department, including support and technical staff, representatives of undergraduate and postgraduate students and research staff. It will in addition spend a good deal of its time in private discussion of the various aspects of a department's work and will, where appropriate, visit laboratories and research rigs. On the final afternoon of its visit the panel will meet with the departmental board, will invite supplementary points from the floor and will lay out, in summary, the outline of its findings and the main points of its report.

Drafting of the report is now the responsibility of the panel's secretary and it will be a brief, 3,000-word account of the visit and an analysis of the department's perceived strengths and weaknesses, mixing, where appropriate, commendations with recommendations for action. A draft will be sent for comment to each member of the panel, with the consequent sub-editing normally being undertaken by the administrative coordinator of the whole ADAP programme in order to ensure a measure of conformity between the various reports, of which, in a typical year, there may be as many as 15. Finally, when the panel has reached its consensus and the report has been finalized, it is sent to the department for it to append its own comments. The joint committee will then meet with the head of department and will have before it the 'profile', the panel's report and the department's reactions to the latter. An hour's discussion will lead to the committee's own report to senate which will normally endorse the panel's recommendations and may append its own, as a consequence of its discussion with the departmental head. Senate will receive this report and will act as the conduit through which recommendations are passed outwards to the appropriate university committees, such as the library committee or staff policy committee, depending upon the nature of the recommendations made. (Comments made by a panel about a department's research standing have also been available to the University management committee at the time the latter considers bids for research initiative funding.) The last part of the whole exercise involves the committee, after perhaps a year's interval, monitoring the implementation of whatever recommendations had been made and, where appropriate, lending its weight to progress any recommendations which have not borne fruit.

Two Brief Case Studies

During a period when universities are being required to make regular so-called 'efficiency gains', it is unrealistic to expect that the outcome of any self-assessment exercise will be a large inflow of university funding to the department concerned. The joint committee is more concerned to ensure that resources, of personnel, equipment, space and money, are used with maximum effectiveness. An ADAP report is also only a 'snapshot' of a department taken and exposed at a particular point in a five-year cycle and it would be invidious for the University to use this as the basis for a transfusion of funds at the inevitable expense of other departments which had not undertaken self-assessment in that particular session. Accordingly the benefits to a department cannot be measured by, say, the number of new Lecturer A appointments it was able to make or the purchase of an expensive piece of equipment.

The value of self-assessment, therefore, needs to be sought in less obvious areas and one such area would be the way in which a department manages and prioritizes its research activities. In Spring 1992 one of our departments was recommended by the panel to 'consider the desirability of presenting its research projects in conformity with UFC expectations'. When in the following year the joint committee monitored the implementation of this particular recommendation it was told that the department had 'reorganised the presentation of its research achievements and plans for the Research Selectivity Exercise, and [had] received a Grade 5'. The value of moving from a Grade 4 to the top-rated Grade 5 is considerable in terms of funding and the potential accession of research grants and postgraduate students, and the department's response certainly indicated that it saw a connection between the self-assessment exercise and its progress from a '4' to a '5'.

In another case – the rehabilitation unit in the faculty of Medicine – the upshot of an ADAP visit had an immediately beneficial effect, as reported by the head of the unit to the joint committee's monitoring of the outcomes of assessment:

Following the Report of the Panel, the group held an 'awayday' on 10 April 1992 facilitated by [the Director of Teaching Support and Media Services]. We went off-campus...[and] reflected on the experience of the assessment and the issues it had raised, identified a need for more regular meetings in the department and a wider and more systematic programme of discussions about day-to-day events in the group and feedback from conferences attended. A fortnightly news sheet is [now] produced...[and] three working parties were established – one on Management, one on Teaching and one on Research – to make recommendations and to feed back to the group as a whole at our monthly Friday meetings. [Another] of our decisions was to have an annual awayday and the next one was held ... on 28 October 1993.

The head of the unit's comments are a powerful tribute to the efficacy of the self-assessment process for without the stimulus provided by the panel's visit and its resulting report it is unlikely that any of these activities would have taken place quite so soon.

Conclusion

In other, more general ways the activities of the joint committee and of its sub-committee on teaching have benefited an institution that has committed itself both to the delivery of high-quality teaching and to the prosecution of internationally-recognized research. For example, a standard student questionnaire has been devised, to which individual departments are encouraged to 'bolt on' a few extra 'customized' questions, and this has been widely used in the annual student evaluation of courses. Central funding has been made available for a teaching and learning developments grant scheme, for which departmental bids are solicited annually. Promotion procedures have been modified to increase the likelihood that promotion will be awarded to a lecturer on the basis of verifiably outstanding teaching; and the University's standard CV form has been redesigned to include evidence of teaching ability as well as of research activity. A timetable has also been established in each faculty whereby each course is subject to annual student evaluation as well as to a full five-yearly review by staff. These developments and such others as the recent establishment of an 'Academic standards committee' have ensured that the University is well-placed to respond to the constantly changing landscape of quality control in higher education and to demonstrate to external providers its shrewd husbandry of public funds.

It would be wrong, however, to end this account by suggesting that the University's self-assessment procedures have now been set in stone. On the contrary, they are constantly changing as we benefit every year from the experience of a further round of assessments. Thus last year we established a working dinner on the eve of the panel visit to permit the external adviser to meet informally with the chair of the panel to map out the ground for the forthcoming visit. This year, similarly, the 'Notes of guidance' which underpin the whole self-assessment process have been thoroughly revised to enable departments to prepare for the HEFCE's assessment of teaching quality at the same time as they are satisfying the University's own internal demands. The University of Southampton's ADAP procedures have undoubtedly been a success for the first five years of their life and have aroused a good deal of national and international interest. However, like any species, they must be prepared to modify themselves in response to external stimuli.

Bibliography

Abbotts, R., Birchenough, M. and Steadman, S. (1988) *GRIDS School Handbooks*, (2nd ed), Primary and Secondary Versions, York: Longman.

Altrichter, H., Posch, P. and Somekh, B. (1993) *Teachers Investigate their Work*, London: Routledge.

Attwood, M. (1986) *Introduction to Personnel Management*, London: Pan.

Balano, R. M. (1994) 'The 10 Commandments of Quality', *Quality Progress*, January, 41–2.

Barnett, R. (1992) *Improving Higher Education, Total Quality Care*, Buckingham: Open University/SRHE.

Baroness Blatch (1992) 'Investors in People. The Wider Context: Government Policy', Investors in People UBI – CBI Conference Keynote Address.

Barrs, M. (1990) 'Quality strained through Jargon', *Times Educational Supplement*.

Becher, T. (1992) 'Making audit acceptable: A collegial approach', *Higher Education Quarterly*, 46, 1.

Blyton, P. and Turnbull, P. (1992) *Reassessing Human Resource Management*, London: Sage.

British Deming Association (1989) *Deming's 14 Points for Management*, Salisbury: British Deming Association.

British Standard (1987a) *Part O: Principal Concepts and Applications*, London: BSI.

British Standards (1987b) *Part 8: Guide to Quality Management and Quality Systems, Elements for Services*, London: BSI.

British Standards (1992) *Total Quality Management BS 7850: Guide to Management Principles*, London, BSI.

British Standards (1994) *BS EN ISO 9000 – Parts 1, 2 and 3*, London: BSI.

British Standards Institute (1990) *BSI Handbook 22: Quality Assurance*, London: BSI.

Brooks, L. (1992) 'The Holy Grail', *Education*, 179, 19.

Burge, S. E. and Tannock, J. D. T. (1992) 'Quality assurance in higher education', *Engineering Professors' Conference Occasional Paper No 4*, March.

Burrows, A., Harvey, L. and Green, D. (1992) *Quality Assurance Systems: A Review of the Application of Industrial Models to Educational and Training*, Birmingham: QHE.

Camp, R. (1989) *Benchmarking*, Milwaukee: Quality Press.

Caplan, R. (1989) *A Practical Approach to Quality Control,* London: Hutchinson.

Carn (1977 onwards) *Classroom Action Research Network,* Cambridge: Institute of Education.

CCVP (1991) *Academic Audit Unit Report on the University of Southampton,* London: CCVP.

Clement, B. (1993) 'Proving that companies which train, gain', *The Independent,* National Training Awards, 4 February, p.31.

Clutterbuck, D. and Crainer, S. (1990) *Makers of Management: Men and Women who Changed the Business World,* New York: Guild Publishing.

Corrigan, J. P. (1994) 'Is ISO 9000 the path to TQM? Even if it isn't, if can't hurt', *Quality Progress,* 27, 5 33–8.

Crawford, F. (1991) *Total Quality Management,* CVCP Occasional Paper, London: Committee of Vice Chancellors and Principals.

Crosby, P. B. (1979) *Quality is Free,* New York: McGraw-Hill.

Crosby, P. B. (1986) *Quality Without Tears: The Art of Hassle-free Management,* Singapore: McGraw-Hill.

Dale, B. (1993) 'Communal education', *Training for Quality,* 1, 1, 24–8.

Dauber, S. L. and Epstein, J. L (1989) Paper presented at ERA conference, cited in Fullan, M. (1991) *The New Meaning of Educational Change,* London: Cassell.

Deming, W. E. (1982) *Quality, Productivity and Competitive Position,* Boston: Massachusetts Institute of Technology.

Deming, W. E (1988) *Out of the Crises,* Massachusetts: CUP.

DES (1988) *Report of the Task Group on Assessment and Testing,* London: HMSO.

DES (1989) *Planning for School Development,* London: HMSO.

DES (1990) *Performance Indicators in Higher Education: A Report by HMI,* London: DES.

DES (1991a) *Development Planning: A Practical Guide,* London: HMSO.

DES (1991b) *Education and Training in the 21st Century,* London: HMSO.

DfE (1992a) *Reports on Individual Pupil's Progress,* Circular No 14/92, London: DfE.

DfE (1992b) *Initial Teacher Training (Secondary Phase),* Circular No 9/92, London: DFE.

DTI (1991) *Total Quality Management and Effective Leadership. Education and Training for the 21st Century,* London: Department of Trade and Industry.

DTI (1992a) *Total Quality Management and Effective Leadership,* London: Department of Trade and Industry.

DTI (1992b) *Quality Circles,* London: Department of Trade and Industry.

DTI (1992c) *The Quality Gurus,* London: Department of Trade and Industry.

DTI (1992d) *The Enterprise Initiative – Managing into the 90's* (5 Booklets), London: Department of Trade and Industry.

Elliott, G. (1982) *Self Evaluation and the Teacher Parts 1–3,* London: Schools Council.

Elliott-Kemp, J. and Williams, G. L. (1980) *The DION Handbook,* Sheffield: Pavic Publications.

Ellis, R. (1993) 'A British standard for university teaching', in Ellis, R. (ed.) *Quality Assurance for University Teaching,* Buckingham: SRHE/Open University Press.

ENB (1992) *Annual Report,* London: ENB.

Etzioni, A. (1969) *The Semi-professions and their Organization: Teachers, Nurses, Social Workers,* New York: Free Press.

Everard, B. and Morris, G. (1990) *Effective School Management,* London: Paul Chapman.

FEFC (1993) *Assessing Achievement* (Circular 93/28), Coventry: Further Education Funding Council.

Feigenbaum, A. V. (1983) *Total Quality Control,* New York: McGraw-Hill.

Freeman, R. (1993) *Quality Assurance in Training and Education,* London: Kogan Page.

Fullan, M. (1991) *The New Meaing of Educational Change,* London: Cassell.

Fullan, M. and Miles, M. (1992) 'Getting reform right: What works and what doesn't', *Phi Delta Kappa,* 73, 10.

Glasser, W. (1990) *The Quality School,* New York: Harper and Row.

Gleeson, D. and Mardle, G. (1980) *Further Education or Training?,* London: Routledge & Kegan Paul.

Goldsmith, W. and Clutterbuck, D. (1984) *The Winning Streak,* London: Weidenfield and Nicolson

Handy, C. (1981) *Understanding Organisations,* London: Penguin.

Handy, C. (1989) *The Age of Unreason,* London: Arrow.

Harvey, L. and Green, D. (1993) 'Defining quality', *Assessment and Evaluation in Higher Education,* 18, 1, 9–34.

Harvey-Jones, J. (1988) *Making it Happen,* London: Collins.

HEFCE (1992a) *Quality Assessment,* Bristol: HEFCE.

HEFCE (1992b) *Claims for Recognition of Excellent Quality Education on Initial Teacher Training Courses,* Circular 6/92, Bristol: HEFCE.

Henley, M. (1987) in Hopkins, D. (ed.) *Improving the Quality of Schooling,* London: Falmer Press.

Henry, J. and Walker, D. (1991) *Managing Innovation,* Buckingham: OU Press.

Henry, T. (1991) 'Quality counts', *Perspective,* Letchworth, National Association of Inspectors and Educational Advisors, April, no 16.

HEQC (1994) *Checklist for Quality Assurance Systems,* London: HEQC.

HEQC/HEFCE (1994) *Joint Statement on Quality Assurance,* London: HEQC.

Higher Education Quality Council/Division of Quality Audit (1992) *Audit Method and Procedures,* Mimeo, May.

Hills, S. (1991) 'Why quality circles failed but Total Quality Management might succeed', *British Journal of Industrial Relations,* 29, 4.

HMI (1992) *Teacher Training Schedules: 1992–3 Inspection Cycle,* London: HMI.

Holt, M. (1992) 'Control freaks leave no room for quality' *TES,* 28 August.

Howarth, C. I. (1993a) Letter to Vice-Chancellors, 5 November 1993.

Howarth, C. I. (1993b) 'Assuring the quality of teaching in universities', *Reflections on Higher Education,* 5, July.

Hutchins, D. (1990) *In Pursuit of Quality,* London: Pitman.

Hutchins, D. (1992) *Achieve Total Quality,* Cambridge: Business Books, Institute of Directors.

Imai, M. (1986) *Kaizen: The Key to Japan's Competitive Success,* New York: Random House.

Insight (1994) *In My View,* Insight no. 29, Sheffield: Employment Department.

Institute of Personnel Management (1993) *Quality: People Management Matters,* London: IPM.

Investors in People (1993) *Incomes Data Services Study,* 5, 30 May.

Ishikawa, K. (1976) *Guide to Quality Control,* Tokyo: Asian Productivity Organisation.

Ishikawa, K. (1985) *What is Total Quality Control? The Japanese Way,* Englewood Cliffs, NJ: Prentice-Hall.

Jackson, P. and Ashton, D. (1993) *Implementing Quality through BS 5750,* London: Kogan Page.

Juran, J. M. (1988) *Planning for Quality,* New York: McGraw-Hill.

Juran, J. M. (1988) *Juran on Leadership for Quality,* New York: Free Press.

Kanter, R. M. (1984) *The Change Masters,* London: Allen & Unwin.

Kanter, R. M. (1990) *When Giants Learn to Dance,* London: Unwin.

KHGMS (1993) *King Harold Grant Maintained School Vision and Mission Statement,* Waltham Abbey: King Harold GM School.

Koch, H. C. H. (1991a) *TQM in Healthcare,* London: Longman.

Koch, H. C. H. (1991b) *Exceeding Expectation,* Brighton: Pavilion Publishing.

Koch, H. C. H. (1992a) *Implementing & Sustaining TQM,* London: Longman.

Koch, H. C. H. (1992b) *TQM in Public Services,* Brighton, Pavilion Publishing

Koch, H. C. H. (1993) *Making TQM Happen,* Brighton: Pavilion Publishing.

Koch, H. C. H. (1994) *Staff Empowerment through QIT Teamwork,* Brighton: Pavilion Publishing.

Kogan, M. *et al.* (1991) *Evaluation of TQM Projects in the NHS,* first interim report to the Department of Health, Brunel University.

Lewin, K. (1947) in Bell, L. (1989) *Management Skills in Primary Schools,* London:Routledge.

Limb, A. (1992) 'Investors in People: Milton Keynes College, A Case Study', Investors in People UBI – CBI Conference Presentation and Papers.

Loader, C. P. J. (ed.) (1990) *Quality Assurance and Accountability in Higher Education,* London, Kogan Page.

Lopate, C., Flaxman, E., Bynum, E. and Gordon, E. (1969) 'Decentralisation and community participation in public education', *Review of Educational Research,* 40, 1.

McGregor, D. (1960) *The Human Side of Enterprise,* London: Pan.

Management Charter Initiative (1992) *A Guide for Employers and Trainers,* London: MCI.

Marchington, M., Dale, B. and Wilkinson, A. (1993) 'Who is really taking the lead in quality', *Personnel Management,* April.

Maxwell, R. (1984) 'Quality assessment in health', *British Medical Journal,* 13, 31–4.

Mizuno, S. (1988) *Management for Quality Improvement: The Seven New Quality Control Tools,* Cambridge, MA: Productivity Press.

Mortiboys, R. and Oakland, J. (1991) *Total Quality Managment and Effective Leadership,* London: Department of Trade and Industry.

Murgatroyd, S. and Morgan, C. (1992) *Total Quality Management and the School,* Buckingham: Open University Press.

Nayak, P. R. (1992) 'Creating a high performance business', *Industry Week,* September 21.

Oakland, J. S. (1989) *Total Quality Management,* Oxford: Heineman.

Oakland, J. S. (1990) *Total Quality Management, A Practical Approach,* London: Department of Trade and Industry.

Oakland, J. S. (1992) 'Continuous improvement and a new model for TQM', *British Quality Association Newsletter,* March.

OFSTED (1993) *Handbook for Inspection of Schools,* London: HMSO.

OFSTED (1994) *Improving Schools,* London: HMSO.

Ormston, M. and Shaw, M. (1993) *Inspection and the GM School,* GMSC Occasional Paper, Series 2, No 3.

Øvretveit, J. (1992) *Health Service Quality,* Oxford: Blackwell.

Parsons, C. (1992) 'Let's do it to ourselves before they do it to us', *Management in Education,* 6, 2.

PCFC (1990) *Teaching Quality,* London: PCFC.

Pearce, E. (1993) 'A lesson in humility teachers refuse to take', *The Guardian,* 5 June.

Peters, T. (1988) *Thriving on Chaos: Handbook for a Management Revolution,* London: Guild Publishing.

Peters, T. and Austin, N. (1985) *A Passion for Excellence,* London: Collins.

Peters, T. and Waterman, R. (1982) *In Search of Excellence,* London: Harper & Row.

Pidgeon, S. (1992) 'Assessment at Key Stage 1: Teacher assessment through record keeping', in Blenkin, G. M. and Keely, A. V. (eds)

Assessment in Early Childhhood, London: Pitman.

Price, F. (1990) *Right Every Time,* Aldershot: Gower.

Robson, M. (1984) *Quality Circles in Action,* Aldershot: Gower.

Robson, M. (1988) *Quality Circles – A Practical Guide,* Aldershot: Gower.

Sallis, E. (1993) *Total Quality Management in Education,* London: Kogan Page.

Sandwell (1992) *The Applicability of BS 5750 to College Operations: Second Year Report, November 1990 – May 1991,* Sandwell: Sandwell College of Further Education.

SCAA (1994) *The National Curriculum and its Assessment – Final Report (The Dearing Report),* London: Schools Curriculum and Assessment Authority.

Sheppard, A. (1992) Reported in an extract from BS News in Newsfile, *Investors in People,* Sheffield: Employment Department.

Shingo, S. (1985) *The Sayings of Shigeo Shingo. Key Strategies for Plant Improvement,* Cambridge MA: Productivity Press.

Simon, H. (1987) *Getting to Know Schools in a Democracy,* London: Falmer Press.

SSRU (1993) *The 1993 Report on the Student Experience at UCE,* Student Satisfaction Research Unit, Centre for the Study of Quality in Higher Education, University of Central England, Birmingham

Stringer, M. and Finlay, C. (1993) 'Assuring quality through student evaluation', in Ellis, R. (ed.) *Quality Assurance for University Teaching,* Buckingham: SRHE/Open University Press.

Sullivan, M. (ed.) (1991) *Change and Development in the Primary School,* London: Longman.

Tannock, J. D. T. and Burge, S. E. (1992) 'A new approach to quality assurance for higher education', *Higher Education Quarterly,* 46, 1.

Tawney, D. (ed.) (1974) *Evaluation in Curriculum Development: Twelve Case Studies,* Basingstoke: Macmillan.

Taylor, P. (1991) Conference Papers from the Senior Project Leader, Employment Department, Moorfoot, distributed at the 'Practical Steps to Quality Conference' New College, Durham, October.

Taylor, W. (1969) *Society and the Education of Teachers,* London: Faber & Faber

Thomson, C. (1989) 'Monitoring client satisfaction in schools – A marketing activity', *School Organisation,* 9, 2.

Thurley, K. and Wirdenius, H. (1989) *Towards European Management,* London: Pitman.

TQM International (1992) *Quality,* Cheshire: TQM International.

Venables, E. (1967) *The Young Worker at College,* London: Faber & Faber.

Vorley, G. (1991) *Quality Assurance Management,* Maidstone: Whitehall Communications.

Waller, J., Allan, D. and Burns, A. (1993) *A Quality Management Manual,* London: Kogan Page.

Walton, M. (1991) *The Deming Management Movement,* New York: Mercury

West-Burnham, J. (1992) *Managing Quality in Schools,* London: Longman.

Wilkinson, A. *et al.* (1991) 'Total quality management and employee involvement', *Human Resource Management Journal,* 2, 4.

Willie, E. (1992) *Quality: Achieving Excellence,* London: Paul Chapman.

Index